State Under Siege

State Under Siege

Development and Policy Making in Peru

Philip Mauceri

WestviewPress

A Division of HarperCollins*Publishers*

Copyright © 1996 by Westview Press, A Division of HarperCollins Publishers, Inc.

Published in 1996 in the United States of America by Westview Press, 5500 Central Avenue, Boulder, Colorado 80301-2877, and in the United Kingdom by Westview Press, 12 Hid's Copse Road, Cumnor Hill, Oxford OX2 9JJ

Library of Congress Cataloging-in-Publication Data
Mauceri, Philip.
  State under siege : development and policy making in Peru / by Philip Mauceri.
    p. cm.
  Includes bibliographical references (p.) and index.
  ISBN 0-8133-2753-9
  1. Peru—Politics and government—20th century. 2. Political planning—Peru.
3. Peru—Economic policy. 4. Peru—Social policy. 5. Power (Social sciences)—Peru.
6. State, The. I. Title.
JL3431.M38 1996
320.985—dc20   **04265904**   96-20662
                                                                                                     CIP

The paper used in this publication meets the requirements of the American National Standard for Permanence of Paper for Printed Library Materials Z39.48-1984.

10   9   8   7   6   5   4   3   2   1

For My Parents

Contents

Tables

Preface

After having been overlooked or dismissed for decades, the concept of "the state" has become central in most works of comparative politics. Almost no analysis of comparative political phenomena is now written without at least mentioning the state's role, policies, or capabilities. Scholars carrying out cross-national studies in state formation or state-society relations have engaged in solid middle-level theory building.

This book hopes to contribute to these efforts through an important case study. States are very much a product of their specific historical experiences and interactions with their societies and thus lend themselves to a case study approach. The focus of this study is a country that has undergone some of the most dramatic changes in state capabilities in Latin America. Through an empirically grounded case study, it examines the factors that influence state capabilities and how they change over time.

The introductory chapter presents the theoretical framework used throughout my analysis. The remainder of the book is divided into two sections. In Part I, I examine the effects of popular mobilization and economic crisis on state development between 1968 and 1995. Chapter Two focuses on the divisions provoked in the military institution by state-initiated mobilization and its gradual loss of control of the mobilization project to radical anti-system opposition groups. This new radical opposition had an important impact on economic policy making, significantly limiting the policy options of economic planners and forcing the state into a constant swing between different and inconsistent economic policies. In Chapter Three, I examine the role of international financial actors in Peru. The search for external financing to deal with economic crises created new vulnerabilities in the international arena. Chapter Four examines the García administration (1985–1990), and specifically the impact of state populism on state capabilities and resources. Overall, the effect of state populism was highly negative, reducing Peru's leverage internationally and dramatically increasing clientelism and corruption in the state apparatus. The legacy of that experience was a level of economic chaos and political instability that left most social actors desperately searching for order. The Fujimori regime quickly fulfilled that wish for many, although

at the cost of greater authoritarianism. In Chapter Five it is argued that the Fujimori regime embarked on a program to reconstruct state power and expand the capabilities of the Peruvian state as a response to the crises of the previous two decades. Whether this project will succeed over the long term remains to be seen, but it nonetheless illustrates how state capabilities must be viewed in the context of changing societal and international forces.

In Part II, I turn my attention to the relation between state power and social policy. Chapter Six looks at an important shantytown district in Lima as it was transformed from a corporatist experiment into a bastion of opposition activity. Villa El Salvador illustrates how effectively societal organizations were able not only to impede authoritarian impositions from above but to use state resources to advance their own goals. For close to two decades, state intervention had the ironic effect of increasing the complexity of this one community. Not all new political organizations that emerged during the 1970s, however, were as positive or benign. Chapter Seven examines the development of the insurgency of Sendero Luminoso and its stunning success during the 1980s in filling "vacuums of power" throughout the countryside. Efforts to combat Sendero are examined in Chapter Eight, which argues that the counterinsurgency campaigns of 1981–1990 demonstrated the serious gaps and weaknesses in state-society relations in Peru. Finally, Chapter Nine draws some comparative implications of this study for other countries in the region.

The process of writing and researching this book has taken close to a decade, and there are many people during that period who helped to motivate, inform, and inspire me. Alfred Stepan and Douglas Chalmers at Columbia University patiently guided my initial steps in this project, while my friends and cohorts at the Institute of Latin American and Iberian Studies at Columbia provided support and a critical ear. I owe a large debt of gratitude to many Peruvian friends and colleagues, particularly at the Instituto de Estudios Peruanos where I was a visiting scholar during 1987 and again between 1988 and 1990. Among the many people whose conversation and criticisms helped me formulate and refine my ideas were Julio Cotler, Romeo Grompone, Aldo Panfichi, Fernando Rospigliosi, Carlos Iván Degregori, Fernando Tuesta, Michel Azcueta, Juan Granda, Cynthia McClintock, Max Cameron, and Jo-Marie Burt. I especially appreciate the support and criticisms of Carol Wise, whose comments on earlier versions of the text were very helpful. I also must thank the librarians at the Universidad Católica, the Biblioteca Nacional, and the Centro de Estudios Históricos-Militares, whose assistance was invaluable. The Graduate College and the College of Social and Behavioral Sciences at the

University of Northern Iowa generously provided funds to prepare the final manuscript.

Finally, I am thankful for the support and inspiration of my wife, Miryam Antúnez de Mayolo, who has been my source of strength as this book took shape.

Philip Mauceri

1

Introduction:
State Power and Policy Making

The Plaza Dos de Mayo in downtown Lima is usually bustling with street vendors and decrepit buses carrying people to and from Lima's outlying shantytowns. On a summer January morning in 1988, however, several hundred persons had nearly filled the plaza. They had gathered in front of the headquarters of the Confederación General De Trabajadores del Perú (CGTP), where they shouted anti-government slogans. The CGTP had called this demonstration during what would be the first of five national strikes in 1988 to protest a series of government austerity packages. Yet the events of the day would make this more than just another anti-government protest. As union leaders and United Left politicians denounced the government of President Alan García, a group of some fifty persons marched into the plaza shouting the slogans of the Maoist guerrilla group, Sendero Luminoso: *"Viva la Guerra Popular! Viva Presidente Gonzalo!"* Within seconds, dynamite exploded behind the crowd and people began to run in terror. Amid the panic and confusion, the intruders quickly moved toward the center of the plaza, firing their pistols into the air. As they did so, armed members of the Communist Party ran out of the CGTP headquarters with their own weapons, surrounding their leaders and firing at the *senderistas*. While the two groups exchanged fire, the police stood by, apparently unwilling to get involved. The ensuing street battle lasted several minutes until the *senderistas* dispersed down nearby streets.

For many Peruvians, the events of that day came to symbolize one of the key problems facing their country: violence and the inability of the state to guarantee basic public order. As insurgent forces expanded, the state seemed unable, and at times even unwilling, to confront these groups. State policy makers also seemed unable or unwilling to confront

1

the country's recurring economic crises. State responses to the economic crisis alternated ineffectually from orthodox to heterodox policies, as the debt burden increased, production declined, and the national income plummeted. Meanwhile, state resources themselves declined precipitously as a result of a dwindling tax base and hemorrhaging public enterprises.

This book will examine the factors contributing to changing state capacities in Peru from the Velasco military regime (1968–1975) through the Fujimori regime of the 1990s. The military regime set into motion the most sweeping set of socioeconomic changes in Peru's recent history. Through the agrarian reform program, the country's traditional land-based oligarchy was virtually eliminated. Union and peasant organizations expanded exponentially, and the industrialization fostered by import substitution policies greatly increased the role of the urban working classes. Urbanization, which had been taking place since the 1950s, turned into a flood that overwhelmed the cities.

The changes begun during that regime created new challenges, conflicts, and limitations for a historically limited state. First, these changes gave rise to new radical political movements, both electoral and armed insurgent, that through the 1980s effectively challenged state prerogatives, strained state resources, and exacerbated conflicts and contradictions within the state and between the state and society. Second, the developmentalist economic model adopted in the early 1970s created a series of internal and external vulnerabilities, notably a large debt and an expanding state sector, which led to serious tensions between business elites, government leaders, and international financial organizations. The policies of successive governments, both authoritarian and democratic, appeared only to exacerbate this situation. Policies adopted to deal with the economic crisis and counterinsurgency contributed to a growing polarization in society, increased Peru's isolation in the international arena, and reduced the resources and capabilities of the state bureaucracy. By the early 1990s a new search for order led to a regime intent on restructuring and strengthening the state apparatus, even if this meant sacrificing democratic norms and institutions.

Before examining these issues, it is important to be clear about what I mean in discussing the state. Following Max Weber, I use the concept of "the state" to indicate that set of administrative and legal institutions that claim "compulsory jurisdiction" over a given territory, maintain "continuous operations," and monopolize the legitimate use of force. Generally this definition has meant that statehood requires a historical and geographic continuity, a military able to maintain the monopoly on the use of violence, and an administrative apparatus that through legal codes and fiscal and tax policies is able to maintain a compulsory jurisdiction over its territory.[1] Although the state as a concept has been criticized as ambiguous and susceptible to multiple, often contradictory, definitions, its persistent use and analytical usefulness argue for the importance of the concept, even at the cost of some conceptual ambiguity.[2] The value of the Weberian approach is that it allows the analyst to examine concrete institutions and norms that, despite social and economic transformations over time, have a certain continuity in historical terms.

State Power and Capabilities

The literature on the state that has emerged over the last two decades provides a rich new framework for an analysis of political change. Much of that literature has focused upon state power. How one understands state power clearly depends upon the defining characteristics assigned to the state.[3] The Marxist approach has largely focused on the patterns of class alliances that support a particular state apparatus and give it defining characteristics. The characteristics of the state are defined by the demands of a particular economy. The problem of state strength or weakness in the orthodox Marxist perspective is thus a matter of the capacity of a dominant class alliance to impose its will on society through the bureaucratic structure of the state. Neo-Marxists, however, concede that state elites are more than just tools for the ruling class(es), and thus may acquire a "relative autonomy" relative to these classes. Nonetheless, state autonomy is limited by the demands of capital accumulation, which tend to undermine state autonomy in the long run.[4] A common critique of the Marxist approach is its difficulty in defining the state in institutional terms, beyond the notion of the state as a mere expression of economic domination. States bring with them historical baggage that is the result of a long history and is linked to cultural and national factors that are not discarded with the passing of a particular economic phase. The institutional arrangements of a state are therefore more than just the expression of a dominant class or economic stage.

Another approach is offered by Joel Migdal, who defines state power in relational terms. For Migdal, state power reflects the capacities of the state to influence and control society, and specifically the capacity to regulate social relationships and extract or use resources in ways the state itself decides.[5] In his analysis of Third World state-society relations, Migdal finds that virtually all states are stymied in their attempts to control and regulate complex societies, where social groups ignore or circumvent the dictates of a distant and uncomprehending state bureaucracy. To a large degree, this is the result of the nature of societies in the

Third World, which he characterizes as composed of a "melange of social organizations" where groups are heterogenous and mechanisms of social control are numerous and widely distributed. Under these conditions, the state is at a disadvantage in its efforts to control society:

> the capacity of states (or incapacity, as the case may be), especially the ability to implement social policies and to mobilize the public, relates to the structure of society. The effectiveness of state leaders who have faced impenetrable barriers to state predominance has stemmed from the nature of the societies they have confronted—from the resistance posed by chiefs, landlords, bosses, rich peasants, clan leaders ... through their various social organizations.[6]

The only "strong" state—that is, a state capable of a high level of social control—which Migdal finds in the Third World is Israel, largely due to its war economy and close-knit religious identity. Even powerful bureaucratic states such as Mexico are seen as unable to regulate social relations effectively. Though Migdal's analysis is aimed at correcting a trend of seeing strong states virtually everywhere, he appears to err at the other extreme. The litmus test that he sets up is one that few First World, let alone Third World states, can pass. Moreover, although societal groups may adapt to state penetration, Migdal pays scant attention to the ways states adapt to societal resistance. As we shall see in Chapter Five, during the Fujimori period there has been a clear attempt to "retool" the state, improving a variety of capacities weakened over the previous two decades and devising new mechanisms of social control that assure continued dominance. The fact that only one state fits in Migdal's "strong" state category raises the question as to whether the criteria for what constitutes strong or weak states are excessively rigid. Is the ability to control and reshape society the only way to measure state power, or are there other power relations that need to be examined to evaluate state power?

An alternative to the unidimensional power relation set up by Migdal would be one that emphasizes a series of state capacities besides social control. Rockman suggests a functional approach focusing on the three capacities of the modern state: production, decision making, and intermediation. He argues that this focus "brings together the most important macrolevel connections of the polity, the society and the economy that cannot be adequately analyzed in isolation from one another."[7] Perhaps the most comprehensive argument regarding the need to focus on a multiplicity of power relations in evaluating state power is presented by Skocpol in her analysis of states and revolution. She notes the need to study states "in relation to socioeconomic and sociocultural contexts," by evaluating state resources and capacities in relation to both national and transnational actors.[8] Here we find one of the most important differences with analysts such as Migdal, namely the addition of an international dimension in state capacities. Transnational factors are considered "key contextual variables" in the determination of state capacities. States do not operate in a vacuum but interact with other states within specific international state systems and also within the structures of a world capitalist economy. Those interactions are never precisely the same Skocpol suggests but vary according to the specific world-historical time framework. A clear understanding of state activity and its limits thus requires understanding these contextual variables. This is especially relevant to Third World states that are particularly vulnerable to economic decision making in advanced industrial states and the international financial system. The limitations faced by officials setting economic policy in a context where interest rates are set in New York and Tokyo and where transnational corporations can and often do use their influence with the industrialized governments to bring pressure on recalcitrant policy makers in Lima, Nairobi, or Manila, clearly involves an important power relation for all Third World states.

In analyzing the role of states in social revolutions, Skocpol suggests that the sources of state power lie in the state's ability to carry out basic administrative and coercive functions.[9] This provides us with a realistic way to begin to evaluate state power. But what exactly are those functions? Here Skocpol is less helpful, pointing us only toward the maintenance of internal order, the ability to compete with other states, and the perpetuation of the state apparatus. In part, the lack of specificity is intentional. State capacities are not fixed but depend upon the particular mix of class structure, the economy, and the international context. There are many relevant questions that emerge in evaluating state capacities. How well can a state defend the integrity of its territory against external and internal challenges to its authority? Does a state possess sufficient financial resources to carry out its functions? Do state agencies possess technically capable staff, and is there a high degree of internal unity and cohesion among state elites, such as in the command of the armed forces? Are groups in civil society compelled to follow state policy, or are policies set by the state largely evaded by affected groups?

Skocpol's approach thus forces the analyst of state power to evaluate a variety of state capabilities, including its own organizational capacities, its influence over society, and its relation with other states. Throughout this study, state power will refer to the state's ability to carry out its basic coercive and administrative functions in these arenas. The effectiveness of the state's capabilities is the key determinant of state strength. Strong states are those whose capacities are utilized effectively, while weak states

suffer from low levels of efficiency and effectiveness. State strength has little to do with size (such as the number of people working in state agencies), brute force (such as the number of people the police can eliminate), or formal prerogatives that cannot be enforced or that lack legitimacy.

Although this approach offers a comprehensive understanding of state power, it presents a serious research challenge given the number of variables involved. Moreover, state power is not fixed in time. Each power relation may vary as a result of changing circumstances. Events since 1989 in Eastern Europe and the former USSR underscore how quickly these changes may take place, and exactly how difficult it is to evaluate state power. Powerful, supposedly totalitarian states, crumbled quickly. Nonetheless, the processes that altered state capabilities in the "totalitarian" East had been underway for some time, as internal capabilities, influence over society, and power relations in the international arena were all dramatically altered during the 1980s.[10] Clearly, there are no set quantitative measures of state power. Since the nature of the variables that determine state power change over time, the analyst is forced to evaluate these multiple factors across world historical time, focusing on continuities and changes in capabilities and contexts.

State Power and Policy Making in Peru

In this book I argue that policies adopted by the Peruvian state from the early 1970s through the late 1980s helped undermine state power. I focus on the interplay between social and economic policies and specific state capabilities. Ironically, two sets of policies emphasized—political mobilization and economic development—were part of the developmentalist state-building effort. Many of these policies were poorly designed or inadequately implemented. Moreover, state agencies undertook new interventionist policies in the economy and society, even as the effectiveness of their policies were diminished by the international environment and the activities of new social actors. The failures of both developmentalist and neoliberal policies during the 1970s and 1980s ultimately paved the way for the restructuring of state capabilities during the 1990s.

Throughout this study, policies are evaluated in the three arenas of state power discussed earlier: (1) the organizational arena, (2) the international arena, and (3) the state-society arena. In discussing the impact of policy making on state capabilities in Peru, it is important to emphasize the historical context of this process. The Peruvian state has been a historically weak state. As we shall see below, capabilities and resources have traditionally been minimal in each power arena during most of the country's history. The developmentalism of the 1960s and 1970s, therefore, represented a major break from the historical pattern of state development in Peru. The difficulties encountered by policy makers wanting to reverse this situation, particularly from social and political actors with a stake in low state development, was not surprising. Moreover, given the unprecedented nature of the changes introduced, it was perhaps inevitable that policy makers would be overwhelmed by the consequences, both domestic and international, of their choices. A brief review of the key policy choices examined in each power arena will illustrate the dramatic changes in state development that occurred during this period.

The State Organizational Arena

My analysis of organizational capabilities focuses on two of the most fundamental aspects of modern state organization. The first is the ability to regulate the economy and administer its own economic resources through fiscal and monetary policies. The development of the modern state is closely linked to its ability to collect taxes and administer the control of the supply of money, tasks that in Western Europe emerged after centuries of arduous and uncertain struggles between kings and nobles, politicians and peasants.[11] With industrialization and the prevalence of Keynesianism, the role of the state took on an added regulatory dimension. Peru, like many developing states, has historically had low fiscal and monetary capabilities. Until 1963 taxation, perhaps the most basic economic function of the state, was carried out by a privately contracted firm.[12] Effective control over monetary policy by the state is similarly a recent phenomenon. The directors of the central bank (BCR) were, until 1969, appointed by the country's business sector—mostly private banks and business associations such as the Mining Society.[13] Thus the BCR, which had been founded only in the middle of this century, was effectively a representative of the interests of economic elites. Policies on such key economic issues as inflation, interest rates, and the money supply were made directly by the business sector in a stunning example of the lack of state autonomy.

This traditionally weak economic policy-making structure was altered throughout the 1960s and in the early 1970s by the Belaúnde (1963–68) and Velasco (1968–75) governments, both of which created new public agencies and enterprises as well as laws and regulations allowing the state to intervene in a variety of economic activities. After the mid-1970s, these state-building efforts began to falter as a result of a growing economic crisis and pressures on the state by newly mobilized popular sectors. Pressures "from below" resulted in sharp swings in economic policies with a tendency toward populist measures to avoid social conflict. The cumulative effect of these policies was to create growing inefficiencies in the state sector, including enterprises that drained resources and a state bureaucracy plagued by corruption and clientelism.

The second element of organizational capacities examined here relates to the effectiveness and cohesiveness of security forces. In nineteenth-century Peru, the military was one of the few state institutions to have both national reach and authority, as well as a centralized organizational structure. In the aftermath of independence the military, as the only centralized and organized institution of the state, dominated the country's politics. Until the emergence of General Ramón Castilla in the 1830s, Peru was governed by a series of military caudillos, whose average period of rule was less than a year. The military's position was also enhanced by persistent border wars, most notably the War of the Pacific with Chile in 1879. Yet internally, the military remained divided between warring caudillos who fought for political advantage and intervened in politics throughout the early twentieth century to support the established oligarchic order. This pattern was only altered by the growing professionalization of the armed forces in the 1950s and 1960s. Reforms were introduced to strengthen the military as an institution, as well as enhance its technical capacities. For this latter purpose, a new military school of advanced learning was created that, as we shall see, had far reaching consequences.

By the late 1970s the professionalization and internal cohesion of the armed forces was seriously challenged. The popular mobilizations initiated by the Velasco regime deeply divided the military institution, and led to the development of factions linked with civilian allies. The military was further divided by the emergence of Sendero Luminoso a decade later. Conflicts developed within the military over strategy and tactics, as well as over the question of civilian control of institutional prerogatives. As these debates occurred, Sendero advanced militarily and politically, exposing the organizational weaknesses of the armed forces.

The International Arena

As an underdeveloped nation, Peru's position in the international arena has always been precarious. Its reliance on traditional exports, primarily minerals, sugar, and cotton, has made the economy extremely dependent on world trade patterns. Foreign ownership of much of the country's economic base has been a constant throughout the nineteenth and twentieth centuries. By the late 1960s over seventy percent of mining production was controlled by foreign, mostly U.S., corporations, and international banks owned most of Peru's commercial banks. Altogether, it was estimated that in fifteen manufacturing sectors, fifty percent of the firms were foreign controlled.[14]

The Velasco regime, heavily influenced by the United Nations Economic Commission on Latin America (ECLA) and dependency theorists, attempted to reverse this situation through nationalizations of foreign enterprises, import-substitution policies, and the expansion of the public sector. Such measures changed the nature of Peru's dependent situation but not its dependency. By weakening the financial base of the state at a moment of world recession, these policies exposed Peru to a greater reliance on international financial institutions. From the mid-1970s onward, successive administrations were repeatedly forced to adopt economic policies that conformed to the prescriptions of international lending agencies in order to secure needed funds. Although attempts were made to resist or alleviate orthodox policy prescriptions by adopting populist measures to deal with rising social demands, such efforts were eventually abandoned. Indeed, the swings from orthodox to populist policies and back and the haphazard ways in which both sets of policies were implemented, only accentuated instability. As we shall see, the single attempt to openly resist international lenders, during the García administration (1985–1990), resulted in a deepening of the country's economic crisis and international isolation.

Peru's experience since the early 1970s in the international arena suggested the difficulties a Third World state confronts when it attempts to change its structurally weak international position. By the start of the Fujimori regime in 1990, few Peruvians were willing to continue challenging international financial actors. The lesson appeared to be that an underdeveloped state must remain subordinate in the international arena to maintain its access to economic assistance and cooperation.

The State-Society Arena

An important indicator of state influence in society is the level of control exercised over social organizations. In Latin America, the state has traditionally had an active role in social organization, primarily through corporatist mechanisms. The prevalence of state corporatism, many have argued, is the result of a strong state apparatus willing and able to intervene in society in order to reshape it, as well as the weakness of political and social actors.[15] The success and durability of corporatist organizations has varied, with its most lasting impact felt in Mexico and Brazil. Corporatism has had less of an impact on those countries with a legacy of strong political parties and weak state organization, such as Colombia and Uruguay.

In evaluating state influence in society, I will be looking at the state's capacity to organize social groups and its ability to influence non-state organizational efforts. The reformist military of General Juan Velasco Alvarado undertook a program to encourage political mobilization among popular sectors. State initiated mobilization is a rare phenomenon. As Trimberger has noted, regimes which undertake structural "revolutions from above," such as those of Ataturk or Nasser, rarely involve state directed mobilization. In the case of Egypt, Nasser created a political party specifically to channel mobilization into support for his regime.[16] To a large extent, the rarity of state directed mobilization is explained by the difficulty of bureaucratic organizations to gain and maintain the loyalty of newly mobilized sectors. What results is what Stepan termed a "control" dilemma: a state can mobilize groups but then cannot control the political activities or orientations that emerge among those groups.[17] This is precisely what occurred in Peru.

While state initiated mobilization may be rare, state policies which have the effect, most often unintended, of significantly mobilizing popular sectors, are not so rare. One of the most common examples involves agrarian reform. Since the late 1950s, a variety of land reforms have been implemented across Latin America by conservative as well as reformist regimes attempting to forestall revolutionary demands. Invariably, such efforts (with the exception of the revolutionary situation in Cuba) have met with the demands of peasants encouraged and emboldened by reforms to pressure for more radical measures, testing the limits of state resolve and power.[18] In essence, agrarian reform highlights differences in class interests and heightens class identity and solidarity by accentuating conflict. The radicalization which results from these reforms, however, may not always be enduring. The way the state responds, if at all, to radicalization has an important impact. A reversal of agrarian reforms, repression, cooptation, or a mix of these responses, may be sufficient to halt peasant radicalization.[19]

During the Velasco period, new social organizations emerged with an anti-state orientation. These groups, including leftist political parties, challenged and took over the corporatist organizations set up by the military regime. The result was the collapse of the state's corporatist project. By the late 1970s not a single corporatist organization set up by the government survived as a pro-regime organization.

State influence in society goes beyond its ability to reshape and organize different social groups. It also must encompass the ability to meet revolutionary challenges to its authority. In the 1980s the Peruvian state faced a growing insurgent challenge that it was unable to effectively confront. An insurgency is a violent armed group that openly contests state power with the goal of replacing the existing state structure with an alternative structure. It does so primarily on the terrain of civil society by gaining the adhesion and loyalty of social groups, attacking the mechanisms of state power, and putting into place the alternative structures that are meant to eventually form the bases of a new state. An ability to repress this challenge and maintain the loyalty of most of society, is a key test of the relative influence and authority of the state in society. The growing strength and influence of Sendero Luminoso in Peruvian society directly challenged state power. Sendero's success in gaining adherents and carrying out armed attacks against its opponents, significantly reduced state capabilities in a wide range of areas.

At the end of 1980s, the rapid deterioration of state capacities had created a growing sense of chaos and even talk of a breakdown of the social order. This sense of crisis and desperation is essential to explaining the ability of the Fujimori administration during the early 1990s to forge a coalition of interests intent on restructuring state power. Supported by the business sector, civilian technocrats, military officers, and international financial organizations, Fujimori initiated a program of reforms directed at strengthening state capacities. But unlike the developmentalism of the 1960s, the new state reform effort was geared toward developing a neoliberal state structure. Thus, while efforts to strengthen state capacities had come full circle, the nature and purpose of that strenthening, as we shall see, was considerably different from previous efforts.

By focusing on the three arenas of state power outlined above, the transition from the end of developmentalism to the rise of the neoliberal state will be highlighted. This transition was uncertain and clearly not linear. The changes in state capacities over the last decades must be seen as a dynamic process responding to shifts in the societal and international contexts within which the Peruvian state operated. It is only by understanding the relations within and between these arenas, that we can begin to explain much of the volatility of Peru's politics.

Notes

1. See Max Weber, "Politics as a Vocation," in H. Gerth and C. Wright Mills, eds., *From Max Weber* (New York: Oxford University Press, 1958), p. 78; and Max Weber, *Economy and Society: An Outline of Interpretive Sociology*, eds., Guenther Roth and Claus Wittich (Berkeley: University of California Press, 1978), p. 56. On the characteristics of the state see J.P. Nettl, "The State as a Conceptual Variable," *World Politics* 20, pp. 559–592.

2. For a discussion of the methodological challenges posed by the state see James Rosenau, "The State in an Era of Cascading Politics," *Comparative Political Studies* 21:1, April 1988, pp. 13–44.

3. An exceptionally clear review of theories of the state is provided by Martin Carnoy, *The State and Political Theory* (Princeton: Princeton University Press, 1984).

4. A very good analysis of neo-Marxist theories of the state, and particularly the issue of autonomy is found in the introduction of Nora Hamilton, *The Limits of State Autonomy: Post-Revolutionary Mexico* (Princeton: Princeton University Press, 1982).

5. Joel Migdal, *Strong Societies and Weak States* (Princeton: Princeton University Press, 1988), pp. 22–25. Migdal's general framework is applied to a series of case studies found in Joel Migdal, Atul Kohli, and Vivienne Shue, eds., *State Power and Social Forces: Domination and Transformation in the Third World* (Cambridge: Cambridge University Press, 1994).

6. Ibid., p. 33.

7. Bert A. Rockman, "Minding the State—Or a State of Mind?: Issues in the Comparative Conceptualization of the State," *Comparative Political Studies* 23:1, April 1990, pp. 25–55.

8. Theda Skocpol, "Bring the State Back In: Strategies of Analysis in Current Research," in Peter Evans, Dietrich Reuschmeyer, and Theda Skocpol, eds., *Bringing the State Back In* (New York: Cambridge University Press, 1985), p. 19. Also see Skocpol's earlier work, Theda Skocpol, *States and Social Revolutions* (Cambridge: Cambridge University Press, 1979).

9. Ibid., p. 29.

10. On some possible answers see Nancy Bermeo, ed., *Liberalization and Democratization: Change in the Soviet Union and Eastern Europe* (Baltimore: Johns Hopkins University Press, 1992); and Martin Malia, "Leninist Endgame," *Daedalus* 121:2, Spring 1992, pp. 57–92.

11. See Gabriel Ardant, "Financial Policy and the Economic Infrastructure of Modern States and Nations," in Charles Tilly, ed., *The Formation of National States in Western Europe* (Princeton: Princeton University Press, 1975), pp. 164–242. Also see the discussion on nation-states and national economies in E.J. Hobsbawm, *Nations and Nationalism Since 1780* (New York: Cambridge University Press, 1990), pp. 27–30.

12. Henry Dobyns and Paul Doughty, *Peru: A Cultural History* (New York: Oxford University Press, 1975), p. 219.

13. David Becker, *The New Bourgeoisie and the Limits of Dependency* (Princeton: Princeton University Press, 1981), p. 256.

14. Laura Guasti, "The Peruvian Military Government and International Corporations," in Cynthia McClintock and Abraham Lowenthal, eds., *The Peruvian Experiment Reconsidered* (Princeton: Princeton University Press, 1983), p. 183.

15. This is a point made by most of the analyses in James Malloy, ed., *Authoritarianism and Corporatism in Latin America* (Pittsburgh: University of Pittsburgh Press, 1977).

16. Michael Hudson, *Arab Politics* (New Haven: Yale University Press, 1977), p. 246.

17. Alfred Stepan, *State and Society: Peru in Comparative Perspective* (Princeton: Princeton University Press, 1978).

18. See Merilee Grindle, *State and Countryside: Development Policy and Agrarian Policy in Latin America* (Baltimore: Johns Hopkins University Press, 1986).

19. Colombia provides an excellent example of this dynamic. See Leon Zamosc, "Peasant Struggles of the 1970s," in Susan Eckstein, ed., *Power and Popular Protest* (Berkeley: University of California Press, 1989), pp. 102–127.

PART ONE

State Development
and Policy Choices, 1968–1995

2

The Military and Popular Mobilization

In July 1977 Peru experienced its first national strike since 1919. What the press termed "Red Tuesday" effectively shut down the country and illustrated the extent of the changes brought about by political mobilization among Peru's popular sectors during the previous decade. Ironically, that mobilization had been promoted and organized by the military, which was then the target of opposition from the very sectors it had mobilized. This chapter focuses on how political mobilization affected the state's organizational capabilities by creating new divisions and challenges for state bureaucracies, especially in economic policy making.

State or state-dependent organizations designed to promote mobilization among popular sectors operated within a context of internal disputes that made the implementation of coherent mobilization policies difficult. These conflicts resulted from the lack of consensus within the military and throughout the state bureaucracy regarding the purpose and goals of mobilization. With such a consensus absent from the beginning, different sectors in the regime used their civilian allies to implement divisive mobilization programs.

In the context of state-sponsored mobilization, various non-state actors with a mobilization agenda of their own began to organize intensively among popular sectors. Sectoral federations, unions, parties, and peasant organizations employed mobilization strategies different from the regime's. These groups concentrated on radical demand-making to acquire and advance their interests. By the end of the Velasco regime, these strategies, already known as *clasismo*, predominated in the labor movement and were gaining increasing strength in other lower-class sectors, such as the peasantry. State-initiated mobilization thus resulted in

the emergence of new anti-system organizations that in later years had increased success.

The disintegration of the military's mobilization project between 1973 and 1975 forced a redefinition of alliances. Over the next two years, the military abandoned its mobilization project and severed ties with those involved. This left the task of organizing lower-class sectors to leftist *clasista* groups. By 1978 the military had entered into a new set of alliances with traditional political groups and embarked on a transition to democracy in order to extricate itself from direct political rule and refocus its efforts on building institutional unity.

Neither Communism Nor Capitalism

The Reformist Coup

During the 1960s important changes occurred in the strategic thinking of the Peruvian military. Because of the rise of guerrilla movements and the experience of the 1962–63 military regime, conceptualizations of national security were refocused away from external threats to the problem of internal threats. Unlike the doctrines developed in the Southern Cone and Brazil during this period, Peru's national security doctrine traced the origins of possible subversive movements to domestic problems arising from socioeconomic underdevelopment rather than to external communist instigation.[1] Throughout the decade, this doctrine was disseminated within the armed forces through the Centro de Altos Estudios Militares (CAEM) and the Army Intelligence School.[2] In these centers, military officials for the first time studied economic development and sociology, analyzing and debating issues beyond military strategies and armaments.

In this context, President Fernando Belaúnde's inability to enact the modest reform program he campaigned for in 1963 created consternation in the military. An APRA-controlled Congress effectively blocked Belaúnde's agrarian reform plans and eliminated any hope for further structural reforms. With the Belaúnde government entering a controversial agreement with the International Petroleum Company in 1968 and the likelihood of a conservative APRA victory in the 1969 elections, the possibility of structural reforms seemed to vanish.[3] On October 3, 1968, the Belaúnde regime was overthrown by a coup, and the armed forces ushered in the "Revolutionary Government of the Armed Forces."

Yet the apparent united action of the armed forces was misleading. The military takeover in 1968 was not an institutional coup. No prior coordination existed among the three branches of the armed forces or between the coup forces and regional military commanders. The president of the Joint Command, General Juan Velasco Alvarado, had only initiated contacts with other officials one day before the actual event. The initiative for the coup emanated from a core group of army officers, primarily colonels and generals who were closely linked to Velasco.[4] With the coup accomplished, negotiations shifted to designing the institutional character of the new regime. Positions within the new junta and in the cabinet were distributed equally among the three branches. The army coup thus became an institutional regime.

The first act of the "revolutionary" regime was to nationalize the International Petroleum Company, whose generous treatment by the Belaúnde government had created a national scandal. This was the first of a series of nationalizations that brought "strategic" economic sectors under direct state control. New state enterprises emerged in the key sectors of the Peruvian economy, such as mining (MineroPerú), fishing (PescaPerú), steel (SiderPerú), petroleum (PetroPerú), and industry (Moraveco). The role of foreign corporations was significantly reduced by the end of the Velasco regime in 1975, while the creation of new state enterprises resulted in significant expansion of the state sector. In 1968, foreign corporations accounted for 33 percent of GDP corporate sector output and the state controlled a mere 16 percent; the remaining 51 percent was controlled by the domestic private sector. By contrast, in 1975 the foreign sector's participation in GDP had been reduced to 17 percent, the state sector's share had increased to 31 percent, and the private sector accounted for 40 percent.[5]

The Velasco regime reshaped rural society by introducing the most profound agrarian reform in Peru's history. The traditional *hacienda* system, which predominated in the Andean highlands and the large export-oriented *haciendas* of the coast, was eliminated by the 1969 agrarian reform, which affected nearly 60 percent of agricultural lands in the highlands and coast.[6] The reform allowed for lands to be reorganized under various schemes including cooperative enterprises or independent associations. In addition, land could be handed over to traditional Andean *campesino* communities, especially if they could demonstrate ancestral links. Altogether, the Peruvian agrarian reform was more drastic and distributed more land than those resulting from either the Mexican or the Bolivian Revolutions.[7]

The implementation of these structural reforms occurred during the most stable period of the Velasco regime (1968–1972), when economic stability and growth prevailed. Within the military, few voices dissented. A growing centralization of decision making in the military took place as the main decision-making channel shifted away from the cabinet and junta toward the presidential advisory group (COAP), largely made up of Velasco's closest advisors. Officers who were identified closely with the reform process were favored, while those opposed were maneuvered into non-critical positions. Yet the question that would divide the military was not the reform program but the decision to implement a policy of political mobilization among popular sectors.

The Mobilization Project

As structural reforms were implemented, a lack of channels became apparent where potential beneficiaries could express their political support or concerns. Unlike issues of economic development and national integration, the question of politically mobilizing lower-class sectors had not been a military concern either before or immediately after the 1968 coup. Thus, no consensus on this issue existed within the core group of officers involved in initiating and promoting reforms.[8] The initial documents of the regime and speeches by high-ranking officers immediately after the coup did not mention mobilization or the problems of political organization. As General Leonidas Rodríguez Figueroa, a major architect of the regime's mobilization policies, noted, "At the beginning of the revolutionary process, no one thought of such things. The participation of the people in the process was talked about, but nothing was done."[9] This conceptual void concerning mobilization meant that unlike the military's reform program, little programmatic consensus existed about what sort of schemes, if any, to adopt.

The first concerted mobilization effort took place in 1971 with the creation of the Sistema Nacional de Movilización Social (SINAMOS). That agency was to promote and support efforts at organizing lower-class groups. The military assumed that the goals and interests of the populace were identical with their own and could be expressed by a military-run agency.[10] SINAMOS advisors were sent around the country to lower-class areas to offer organizational assistance. Advisors played a key role in informing people of their rights under the revolution and used a new radical discourse among the popular class that had only been employed by the extreme left. That discourse emphasized the need for revolutionary change and the exploitation the poor had suffered for centuries.[11] The vast majority of SINAMOS advisors were civilian *tecnicos*. These civilians provided technical expertise and occupied key roles within the SINAMOS system. The agency was designed by a former Aprista intellectual, Carlos Delgado, and prominent center-left intellectuals formed the majority on the SINAMOS advisory board. Because the Velasco regime lacked a clear vision of the role the mobilization project played in the "revolution," it was forced to look outside the military for assistance.

The military confronted two important limitations in implementing mobilization policies. First, there was no programmatic consensus within the armed forces on the need for mobilization among lower-class sectors.

This contrasted with the clear consensus on the need for structural reforms, such as state control of strategic industries. Second, there was no prior thinking about the type of mobilization policies that should be adopted. The mobilization problem was not considered until after the 1968 coup, and the schemes adopted then responded to different motivations and interests. These limitations were only symptomatic of the larger conceptual problem confronting the Velasco regime: how to define the goals and purpose of the Peruvian Revolution.

In 1970, General Velasco declared that the Peruvian Revolution was "neither communist nor capitalist" and referred to many traditions influencing the regime. Although some officials, including Velasco himself, often mentioned the importance of the "socialist" tradition in the revolution's ideology, others pointed to "christian" or "humanitarian" sources.[12]

A clear definition of the regime was not just a question of finding the correct word or concept to express the military's goals. Rather, it meant relating the revolution's goals with the concerns and needs of the poor. If "revolutionary change" was the end goal of the regime, as its leaders and SINAMOS advisors insisted, what advantage was there in a conciliatory "humanitarian" approach over a conflictive, and possibly violent, approach to confront and eliminate opponents of change? As the military implemented its mobilization project, its inability to address these issues became an enormous and fatal handicap.

Conflict and Disintegration, 1973–1975

The Military

Growing differences within the military led to the emergence of distinct factions in the regime, each with its own mobilization agenda and set of civilian allies. From 1973 to 1975, conflicts within the armed forces over the goals of mobilization policy increased dramatically. Also contributing to this new environment was General Velasco's declining health, which seriously limited his capacity to arbitrate disputes.

Soon after SINAMOS began operating in early 1972, a new organization was formed to defend the revolution in the labor sector. The Movimiento Laboral Revolucionario (MLR) emerged in the powerful Chimbote-based fishermen's federation led by Gil Peñaranda. To defend the revolution from what they saw as "communist infiltration," the MLR attempted to gain control of several labor unions around the country. MLR officials were often accused of violently threatening and intimidating their opponents. From the start, the MLR received support from Minister of Fishing General Javier Tantaleán Vanini, who often attended meetings as an official regime representative along with Labor Minister

General Pedro Sala Orosco.[13] Reports often linked the MLR with APRA insofar as their tactics were similar, both used anti-communist rhetoric, and General Tantaleán's own family was connected with APRA.

General Tantaleán and other officers sympathetic to the MLR (referred to as "*La Misión*" by the press) shared a common concern with what they saw as communist infiltration in the mobilization process. Despite this, *La Misión* was more "statist" than conservative, endorsing an expansion of state powers in strategic sectors and the need to control and orient mobilization.[14] *La Misión* also emphasized forming a pro-regime political party and discarding the "no-party" thesis formulated by Carlos Delgado in SINAMOS. According to supporters of this approach, an official party would channel mobilization into effective support for the regime and help combat "infiltration" of the state.

La Misión's orientation and methods sharply contrasted with those SINAMOS promoted and followed in labor communities and agricultural cooperatives. The "progressive" officers most closely identified with SINAMOS' efforts, such as its former director, General Leonidas Rodríguez Figueroa, and General Fernández Maldonado, were less preoccupied with the threat of infiltration from the left. They discarded the need for a political party, emphasizing that the people's support for the regime was a result of the benefits they received from the revolution. In their view, parties were seen as primarily clientelist and opportunist organizations.[15] Yet by late 1973 the progressive position in the regime appeared to be weakening. General Rodríguez was replaced in SINAMOS by the pro-MLR General Sala Orosco, while Velasco himself met with MLR leaders. This perception of the MLR's growing influence was reinforced by an increasingly anti-communist tone in Velasco's own speeches.[16]

In July 1974, Velasco announced the nationalization of the daily press, an act that dramatically intensified conflicts within the military. The MLR favored the nationalization and General Tantaleán had directed the internal commission that studied the issue. Newspapers were one of the few remaining sectors where opposition from the right and left could be expressed. News of meetings, rallies, strikes, and relatively free analyses of the political situation, filled the newspaper pages. The nationalization was, therefore, a clear attempt to increase "control" over the revolutionary process.

Nonetheless, the nationalization almost immediately created a new arena of conflict within the regime. Where newspapers had been vehicles for non-regime actors to express their opposition, the nationalization gave an outlet to regime actors and allies to use "their paper" against opponents. The internal polemics of the regime were now aired publicly through the front pages of the daily press.[17] The daily *Ultima Hora* under Ismael Frias, became a pro-MLR bastion; *Expreso*, owned by its workers, expressed sympathies with the regime-allied Communist Party; and *Correo* and *La Crónica* supported the progressive position in the regime.

Prior to the nationalization, the daily *El Comercio* was one of the few conservative voices left in the country to express concern about the dramatic pace of changes. It was also an important voice for conservative members of the military. For example, Minister of the Navy Vice-Admiral Vargas Caballero through early 1974 issued declarations to the paper on the need to defend "western and christian civilization," a phrase often repeated by conservatives to express concern about mobilization among the popular sectors. In May 1974, Vargas declared that the military had accomplished its mission and should return to the barracks. The next day, at a public press conference, President Velasco demanded the minister's resignation, which was duly submitted.[18]

Vargas' resignation was indicative of the growing opposition in the navy to the rapid pace of changes. Navy officials tended to be from coastal, urban, upper-class white sectors, and traditionally were the most conservative in the armed forces. By contrast, virtually all of the regime's army leaders were from lower or middle-class families, provincial, and *cholo* (mixed or indian) backgrounds.[19] Following Vargas' resignation, four admirals submitted their requests for retirement. Vargas' successors, Vice-Admirals Faura Gaig and Arce Larco, were among the few Velasco sympathizers in the navy and encountered significant resistance to their authority. This situation reached a climax in early 1975 when a petition from several hundred naval officers was circulated demanding the removal of Faura Gaig and implying the possibility of a naval revolt. Faura Gaig was removed in June 1975, effectively avoiding what could have become a major confrontation.

Labor: From Mobilization to Clasismo

The labor sector was a major area of conflict during this period. Political actors ranging from the MLR, SINAMOS, the Communist Party, and Maoists, competed to organize workers and develop dominant union federations. The decline of APRA's control of labor after the 1960s opened the way for new organizational efforts.[20] The main beneficiary of APRA's decline, however, was the Communist Party and not the regime. By 1975, the Communist Party's Confederación General de Trabajadores del Perú (CGTP) was the predominant force in the labor movement.

The importance of organized labor in Peru went beyond its representation in the workforce, which was less than 15 percent. Organized labor was concentrated in the most strategic sectors of the Peruvian economy,

including mining, fishing, industry, and the public sector. Strikes or other actions which paralyzed one or more of these sectors could result in serious economic losses. Despite this importance, the regime initially paid little attention to mobilization policies in the labor sector. Regime policy largely focused on favoring the organizational efforts of the CGTP in the labor sector to counteract the traditional influence of APRA.

The number of labor organizations during the Velasco era dramatically increased. Nearly 2,000 new unions were officially recognized from 1969 to 1975—the same number of unions recognized in the previous thirty years. The vast majority of these new unions affiliated with the CGTP. When the CGTP held its first founding congress in 1969, only a small minority of unions were affiliated. This situation changed rapidly. By 1977, 44 percent of all unions were affiliated with the CGTP, 21 percent with Maoist "New Left" confederations, and 27 percent remained in the Aprista Confederación de Trabajadores Peruanos (CTP).[21] It was only in 1972 that the regime created its own labor confederation, the Confederación de Trabajadores de la Revolución Peruana (CTRP), which played a secondary role to SINAMOS and later to the MLR in the labor sector.

Aside from the acceleration of union recognitions, the regime implemented a variety of new schemes in the labor sector that favored a strong leftist presence. The creation of *comunidades industriales* (CI's) in 1970 and the formation of the Congress of Comunidades Industriales (CONACI) in 1972 opened up a new area of labor activity. Through these organizations, workers shared information, created new publications, and formed solidarity groups. These sorts of contacts were critical in establishing a network of horizontal relations in the labor sector that had not existed under the clientelist system of the Aprista CTP. Far from what had been planned, the implementation of the CI's did not guarantee the military's dominance in this sector. By 1974 the regime had clearly lost control of CONACI. Despite the strong influence of SINAMOS in CONACI, members elected leaders aligned with the CGTP.

The shift towards leftist dominance in the labor movement meant more than new actors in that sector. The CGTP and other leftist groups introduced a new set of labor strategies and identities markedly different from APRA's clientelism or the regime's attempted corporatism. Such tactics were based on radical demand making to assert class-oriented "rights" beyond simple wage issues. *Clasismo* as practiced by the unions, meant the use of *medidas de fuerza* (employing force) to protect and advance member interests and also to instill class consciousness, so workers "personally feel and understand the nature of a society divided into classes."[22] These confrontational tactics included strikes (partial, prolonged, or in solidarity with other unions), marches, rallies, propaganda (leaflets, graffiti, or newspapers), and even violent confrontations with authorities or employers. Confrontational and combative tactics were the primary mechanisms to protect and advance worker interests for *clasista* unions.[23]

The effectiveness of *clasismo* was linked to an expanding range of "rights" and benefits for the labor movement. *Clasista* strategies were especially effective in eliminating the traditional means of enforcing "labor discipline." In 1970, the regime adopted a drastic law of *estabilidad laboral* that prohibited the dismissal of employees after three months, thus eliminating the threat of dismissal for workers engaged in strikes or other radical tactics. To a large degree, the *estabilidad laboral* law made *clasista* tactics not only viable, but in simple cost-benefit terms, preferable over traditional clientelism or the conciliatory corporatism proposed by the regime.

This new combativeness of labor clearly contributed to growing labor conflicts. By 1973 the labor peace that had predominated since 1968, came to an end. The number of strikes between 1973 and 1975 was unprecedented in Peru's labor history and represented a doubling of the levels reached in the previous three year period (see Table 2.1). This increase occurred rapidly—the number of strikes exploded from 409 in 1972 to 788 in 1973. These strikes affected all the major sectors of the Peruvian economy, especially industry and the public sector, where nearly half of the strikes occurred. CGTP affiliates carried out the majority of the strikes, accounting for 63 percent of the man-hours lost to strikes in this period.[24] With another 20 percent led by New Left labor federations, these strikes demonstrated the new power the left exercised in the labor sector.

Adding to this conflictive environment was the organizational competition among different political groups, primarily between SINAMOS, the CGTP, and Maoists. Although the CGTP was officially an ally of the regime, adhering to the Communist Party's policy of *apoyo critico* (critical support) of Velasco, the confederation was nonetheless openly hostile to regime organization in the labor sector.[25] Such hostility translated into open warfare with regime organizations such as SINAMOS, the CTRP, and the MLR. CGTP policy toward SINAMOS was typical. The CGTP considered SINAMOS activity in the labor sector a threat to its own organization and to the *clasismo* it promoted. In an internal evaluation of SINAMOS at its organizational congress, the CGTP decided to combat this danger by orienting workers against SINAMOS, an easy task given the handicaps SINAMOS suffered.

> [Most workers] are tired of the persistent government declarations of 'neither communism nor capitalism.' And that is not because the workers

are either capitalists or communists, but because they prefer to approach things by what they are, and not by what they are not. When SINAMOS promotes these ideas and methods, they generate a natural resistance among the workers. Against this an entire army of bureaucrats with money in their pockets, cars, and secretaries does not constitute a solution.[26]

The conflict between the CGTP and the state was only one side of the organizational competition in the labor sector. An assortment of other leftist organizations, primarily Maoist, competed with both the state and the CGTP.[27] These "New Left" groups accused the CGTP of collaborationism and they claimed to represent the only true opposition to the regime, which they denounced as fascist. Amid the predominance of *clasismo* and the 1973–1975 economic crisis, their message found an increasing audience.

TABLE 2.1   Labor Strikes, 1965–1979

Year	*Number of Strikes*	*Man Hours Lost (millions)*
1965	397	6.4
1966	394	11.7
1967	414	8.4
1968	364	3.4
1969	373	3.9
1970	345	5.8
1971	377	10.9
1972	409	6.3
1973	788	15.7
1974	570	13.4
1975	779	20.3
1976	440	6.8
1977	234	5.0
1978	364	36.1
1979	653	7.9

Source: International Labour Organization, *Yearbook of Labour Statistics* (ILO: Geneva); 1965–69 figures from vol. 30, p. 787; 1970–74 figures from vol. 35, p. 799; 1975–79 figures from vol. 40, p. 635.

By 1974 both the teachers' (SUTEP) and miners' (FNTMM) federations, two of the country's most powerful labor organizations, had elected Maoist leaderships. Moreover, to counteract the influence of the CGTP, the Maoist Patria Roja organized a competing labor confederation, the Comité de Coordinación y Unificación Sindical Clasista (CCUSC). At its peak in 1975, the CCUSC united 664 base organizations under its banners to struggle against "defeatism" and to create a Marxist-Leninist-Maoist Revolution.[28] The growing influence of the New Left did not go unnoticed by the regime. An evaluation by SINAMOS suggested that the "ultra" presence in the labor sector represented "legal, institutionalized, and massive action" that could serve "to raise entire social classes, regions, and cities, against the revolution." The report emphasized the need to combat the New Left influence politically, ominously concluding that "what is at stake is the fate of the entire revolutionary process."[29] Given the later rise and growth of Sendero Luminoso, this appraisal seems quite accurate even though the timing was wrong.

The organizational competition that pitted the state, CGTP, and the New Left against each other for labor's adherence occurred during Peru's first economic crisis since the 1968 coup. That crisis originated in the sharp rise of world petroleum prices; a decline in the price of Peru's major exports such as copper, fishmeal, and textiles; and a balance of payments problem resulting from the previous nationalizations. Inflation and the foreign debt increased, while wages and salaries declined. The previous increases in worker income were eliminated. Real wages had increased 26 percent between 1968 and 1972 but by 1975 they had returned to their 1968 levels.[30] This decline in income, the predominance of *clasista* attitudes, and the radical rhetoric of groups competing to represent workers, made labor conflict almost inevitable. As an increasingly divided regime confronted labor protests, both it and its mobilization project fell into a period of vacuum and chaos.

The Fall into Chaos

As the state-initiated mobilization project collapsed and was replaced by radical anti-system movements, divisions within the military increased. These conflicts reached a crisis level as a result of riots on February 5, 1975. The streets of Lima were unprotected when police went on strike for better wages. Provoked by price rises and the lack of security on the streets, rioting mobs spread out from lower-class neighborhoods such as La Victoria, into the center of the city to loot unprotected stores. The absence of protection was complete. Army troops remained in their barracks until the worst rioting was over.

The riots went beyond mere looting. Offices associated with the regime were a special target of rioting mobs. They destroyed the offices of pro-regime newspapers, sacked a newly inaugurated civic center, and burned down the headquarters of SINAMOS and a military club.[31] Rumors of APRA's involvement in this destruction were persistent, fueled by the vaguely worded communiqué from its leadership claiming "the party as such did not intervene in these events."[32]

The rioting and sacking of government offices as well as the apparent paralysis in the regime's response produced growing concern about a power vacuum at the highest levels. Requests for protection and military action during the rioting went unattended. During and immediately after the riots, regime officials did not make any public appearances. Even more notable was the absence of regime supporters on the streets. State mobilization agencies and groups allied with the regime did not mobilize supporters to defend their institutions. An independent journal sympathetic to the regime summed up the political implications for the mobilization project:

> Where were the thousands of SINAMOS activists? Where were all of us who claim to be partisans of socialism and the Peruvian Revolution? That day (February 5) there was no one to coordinate popular organizations, no one to give instructions for action. That day the tremendous vacuum resulting from the lack of a political organ was demonstrated.[33]

A key factor contributing to the growing sense of the regime's lack of direction was the decline of President Velasco's health. His sickness took a turn for the worse in 1974 and the lack of any succession arrangements created growing preoccupation within the military.[34] Velasco's inability to arbitrate the military's internal conflicts only added to the regime's growing paralysis. Without clear leadership and with the mobilization project in shambles, the diverse tendencies within the regime regrouped around new alternatives. By early 1975, the power of *La Misión* within the military was waning. In part, this reflected the slow decline of the MLR, which was losing its influence in the labor movement.

Despite this setback, *La Misión* appeared to enjoy President Velasco's continued favoritism. Velasco used his Independence Day speech to emphasize the need for control in the mobilization process and combined that with a warning about communist infiltration in the revolution. Following that speech, a new organization was introduced to help meet what was seen as the government's need for control. With the apparent approval of Velasco himself, General Tantaleán announced the formation of a "non-party" party of the revolution: the Organización Política de la Revolución Peruana (OPRP). The word party was strictly avoided in describing the new group, whose purpose was to advance the "ideology and doctrine of the Peruvian Revolution." The corporate structure of OPRP was similar to that of SINAMOS. Participation was through affiliated organizations and not through personal inscriptions.[35] The similarity seemed to signal that OPRP's major competitor would not be the traditional parties but the progressive linked SINAMOS.

Amid the intensification of the internal struggles in the regime, a new position within the armed forces emerged that emphasized the need to reestablish the institutional unity and corporate identity of the military as an institution. This position was most strongly promoted by the Premier, General Francisco Morales Bermúdez, who in early 1975 ascended to the senior institutional rank in the army as its commander general and also assumed the position of president of the Joint Command. The three positions he held made him the most powerful official aside from Velasco and, given Velasco's illness, gave Morales significant decision making power.

As a result, General Morales' growing concern that internal conflicts were dividing and weakening the military took on special importance. In this institutional view, such conflicts politicized the armed forces and distanced it from its mission of national defense and its role as a "tutelary" institution incarnating the nation.[36] This danger of a politicized military and the power vacuum General Velasco's illness caused were the primary reasons behind the coup d'etat of August 29, 1975. In a communiqué issued from the border city of Tacna, General Morales ordered the removal of Velasco from the presidency and his own assumption of that position. The communiqué was issued only after consultations with all of Peru's regional commanders. The 1975 coup, unlike that of 1968, was an institutional coup, involving the full support and a priori consent of the military hierarchy. Putting the action in clear institutional terms, the new government described the removal of Velasco as part of an "institutional movement" of the armed forces and not as a coup either for or against individuals.

As an eloquent testimony of the mobilization project's failure, no public demonstrations of support or protests accompanied Velasco's removal from the presidency. The public plazas were empty of protesting *campesinos*, workers, or shantytown dwellers when Velasco left the presidential palace. Yet, if the mobilization project begun under his regime failed to provide him with a personal support base to continue in power, it did not mean that popular sectors had not been mobilized or that all had returned to the pre-1968 status quo. As the new Morales regime soon discovered, sectors that had been mobilized were now willing and able to actively oppose state policies they disliked.

Redefinitions, 1975–1977

New Oppositions

During the first two years of the Morales regime, political groups formerly allied with the military joined the growing opposition to Morales. Their primary focus was the new conservative economic and social policies which Morales unveiled slowly, as the regime attempted to emphasize continuities with General Velasco. Morales declared that the revolution would continue under his presidency. With the announcement of the first package of conservative economic measures in 1976, the regime adopted the formula of the "first phase" and "second phase" of the revolution to distinguish itself from the Velasco period, noting that sacrifice was required to institutionalize the first phase reforms.

Throughout late 1975 and early 1976, the regime moved slowly to change its internal decision-making processes. This slow pace suggested Morales was more interested in establishing consensus within the new regime before dramatically shifting the military's priorities. In January 1976, a conservative economic program was introduced which included devaluations and a sharp cutback in state spending. Morales argued that a period of austerity was required to "consolidate the revolution." Organizations that had backed Velasco publicly supported Morales' argument, including the Communist Party. With expectations of possible changes in the nature of the regime abounding, most groups outside of the New Left willingly provided the military breathing space.

Several events dramatically changed this situation, including military rebellions from both conservative and progressive sectors. The first rebellion occurred in early July when General Bobbio Centurión, who had previously spoken of the "communist threat," ordered tanks into the streets of Lima's wealthy districts. The action served as an excuse to dismiss the remaining progressive officers. It also provoked a second coup attempt, this time from the left. Led by middle-ranking officers and prominent civilian advisors, a group known as *La Orga* planned to take over a military base and begin a generalized rebellion against Morales Bermúdez. However, the army's intelligence service detected the plan and deactivated it several days before it was to be carried out. A purge of nearly 300 officers involved in the conspiracy followed, along with the deportation of prominent pro-Velasco and leftist civilian leaders.[37]

These rebellions effectively eliminated Velasco-linked sectors in the upper ranks of the military and consolidated the shift toward a conservative regime. Moreover, the conservative position was strengthened with the appointment of General Luis Cisneros Vizquerra as minister of interior and the purge of leftists on newspaper editorial boards. Cisneros cracked down on *Velasquista* and leftist leaders, deporting or detaining over one hundred opposition leaders by the end of the year, including former Velasco Generals Rodríguez Figueroa and Fernández Maldonado. Although the regime's rhetoric continued to emphasize the continuity between "first phase" and "second phase," the changes introduced by the end of 1976 amounted to a change in regime. The talk of different "phases" obscured the fact that the make-up and policies of the Morales regime were fundamentally different from those Velasco followed. This became even more apparent as the military discarded its alliance with groups promoting mobilization and set up new alliances with traditional political groups.

The state organizations involved in promoting mobilization were either disbanded or fell under the control of the opposition. The fate of mobilization agencies depended upon their internal structure and the level of accountability to their members. Bureaucratic and administrative agencies created to promote mobilization (e.g., SINAMOS) were simply disbanded. By contrast, organizations that included elections or member assemblies (CTRP, CNA, CONACI) replaced their pro-regime leaderships with opposition leaders through internal elections.

Meanwhile, the regime-allied Communist Party was torn by a series of internal conflicts that resulted in its definitive break with the military government. From 1975 to 1977 the party and its labor federation, the CGTP, had lost the initiative in labor mobilization to other leftist groups because of their continued alliance with the Morales regime. New Left parties and organizations argued they were the only opposition to the regime and the CGTP's repeated calls for austerity amounted to collaborating with an "anti-worker" regime. The continued marches and rallies called by the Maoist Patria Roja and other New Left groups demonstrated that their message was gaining a wider audience.

The expansion of these groups' influence from 1975 to 1977 is demonstrated in the growth of new popular sector organizations linked to the New Left. The most powerful of these organizations was the Confederación Campesina del Perú (CCP). Originally founded in 1947, the CCP was reorganized in 1974 under the direction of the Maoist Vanguardia Revolucionaria. Between 1974 and 1976, the CCP successfully promoted a series of land invasions among peasants in Andahuaylas (Apurimac), Cajamarca, and Piura, to "radicalize" and extend Velasco's agrarian reform. Since land under the agrarian reform was a "right" conceded to all campesinos, peasants who did not receive land felt justified in carrying out land invasions. State officials usually granted land titles to peasants during the negotiations that would follow an invasion. Thus, the

land invasions were generally an effective way to acquire titles for peasants who would otherwise have not benefitted from the reform.

Activists from the CCP and New Left parties provided technical and
legal assistance throughout the land invasion process, bringing their
experiences from other regions of the country. In most instances, invasions would have failed without such assistance.[38] The CCP and the New
Left carried out the same *clasista* practices used in the labor movement.
Land invasions, like strikes, were measures to assert and protect an
acquired "right" that belonged to peasants as a class (or class fraction).
The *clasista* discourse among peasants, as in urban factories, emphasized
the division of class and the necessity of struggle, as opposed to the
regime's rhetoric of conciliation. Land invasions clearly expanded the
influence of *clasismo* and the New Left beyond the labor movement into
the rural regions of the country. By 1977 the CCP had displaced the pro-
Velasco Confederación Nacional Agraria (CNA) as the largest campesino
federation in the country with an estimated 200,000 members.

The National Strike of 1977

With the progressives removed from power, the regime's shift toward
conservative policies became more pronounced. In February 1977 Plan
Tupac Amaru was issued, outlining the regime's economic goals. As
expected, no new reforms were announced. Immediately following its
publication, President Morales met with the leaders of the traditional
political parties—Luis Bedoya of the Partido Popular Cristiano (PPC),
Fernando Belaúnde of Acción Popular (AP), and Victor Raúl Haya de la
Torre of APRA—and they all expressed their support for the plan. These
meetings were the first in a series with traditional party leaders, breaking
Velasco's isolation and disdain for Peru's parties. The appointment of a
businessman as the first civilian minister of finance since 1968 also sig-
nalled a growing closeness between Morales and the traditional political
elite.

Yet no sooner was a new package of economic adjustments
announced, then the limits on policy making imposed by mobilization
became evident. The price rises and wage freezes sparked riots in the
major cities of the southern highlands, requiring a state of emergency
declaration in Cusco, Puno, and Arequipa. Faced with such protests,
Morales reduced the scale of price rises which resulted in the resignation
of Minister of Finance Luis Barúa. Demands for greater austerity came
primarily from Peru's international lenders. As the economy fell into
crisis after 1973, the military turned to external borrowing to cover its deficits. However, in return for new funds, Peru's foreign lenders, and in
particular the International Monetary Fund (IMF), demanded stricter eco-

nomic reforms. These policies included a reduction in subsidies, price rises, and greater control of state spending and monetary policies.[39]

To confront the growing crisis and meet the demands of the IMF, Minister of Finance Walter Piazza unveiled an economic emergency plan in early June 1977, eliminating subsidies on basic food items such as milk, freezing wages, and further reducing state spending. Piazza was a well-known business leader and his plan met with approval from conservative business sectors and the IMF. Nonetheless, the plan unleashed a wave of protests from popular sectors and the Catholic Church. Although Piazza resigned in early July, his policies set the stage for the largest national strike of the post-war era. The idea of a general strike was raised by the New Left and the Maoist CCUSC as early as 1975.[40] After new negotiations, twenty-three organizations, from union federations to shantytown groups to regional federations, signed an accord calling for a national strike.

A separate declaration was also issued by most of Peru's leftist parties supporting the strike. The absence of a demand for an end to the military regime in all of these documents reflected the political agenda of the Peruvian left. That agenda was based on either a return to the reform process begun by Velasco, as in the case of the Communist Party, or the complete destruction of the Peruvian state, the maximalist goal of the New Left. In either case, a return to procedural democracy was seen as a step backward to the pre-1968 status quo. This would mean a return to traditional political institutions and rules that until 1968 had favored conservative groups. The experience of authoritarian rule in Peru, therefore, had the opposite effect on the left than it had in most of South America during this period. Rather than resulting in a "revaluation" of liberal democratic norms and procedures, the Peruvian experience with authoritarianism reenforced the view that liberal democratic procedures limited the possibility of enacting significant social reforms.[41]

Despite warnings from Interior Minister General Luis Cisneros that harsh action would be taken against strike participants, the strike met with surprising success, effectively shutting down the country for twenty-four hours. This was the first clear demonstration of the new found power exercised by the labor movement and the political left. Not since the 1919 general strike helped overthrow President Billinghurst had there been such a massive protest. By the end of the year the effects of the strike were clear: an acceleration in the regime's cooperation with traditional parties and the business sector, internal changes in the military that favored a return to civilian rule, and increasing efforts in the labor movement and the left to achieve a united leftist opposition front.

Searching for a Transition Formula, 1976–1977

New Alliances and the Military

The national strike of 1977 and what followed in early 1978 accelerated moves toward a transition to civilian rule. The decision to return to civilian rule had already been announced in February 1977 with the release of Plan Tupac Amaru, declaring that general elections would be held in 1980.[42] However, no specific schedule was set for the elections and there were no explicit guarantees that all parties and candidates would be allowed to participate. It was only in late July, a mere ten days after the national strike, that an election schedule finally announced the dates and rules for a constituent assembly election later in the year.

After eliminating the progressive and *La Misión* tendencies within the regime and dismantling the mobilization project, Morales began the last task of the military's "depoliticization"—the transition to civilian rule. A return to civilian rule was the logical outcome of the "institutionalist" position that had overthrown General Velasco. The most direct way to avoid the dangers of a politicized military, so often cited by officials of the Morales regime as a threat to the military institution, was to remove the military from governance.

The return to civilian rule was also consistent with the new alliance between the military and civilians. Having discarded the Velasco alliance with the Communist Party, the CGTP, and other leftist groups, Morales found new allies among traditional political parties and the business sector, both of whom Velasco had shunned. In his 1977 Independence Day speech, Morales unveiled significant changes in the *estabilidad laboral* law and in the labor community scheme of the Velasco regime. Both changes were defended as "readjustments" in labor policies needed to promote greater investment by private enterprises and were widely applauded by the business sector.[43] Morales also opened a series of talks with the leaders of APRA, AP, and the PPC, most of whom had been marginalized or exiled by the Velasco regime. By the time the Constituent Assembly began to function in late 1978, these "consultations" between the military and traditional parties had been converted into full cooperation in governing the country and in guiding the transition to civilian rule.

The conservative economic and social policies followed by Morales reflected the deeper changes in the internal make-up and external alliance system of the military regime. The Morales regime was backed by institutionalist officers and traditional political and economic actors who supported dismantling the Velasco mobilization project and extricating the military institution from direct political rule. As Table 2.2 indicates, the differences between the Velasco and Morales regime involved more than different policy orientations or emphases. Although the "cooperative" relationship established between Morales and traditional groups never resulted in formal pacts, the transition to civilian rule involved intense consultations and negotiations with traditional political parties. Behind the distinction of "first phase" and "second phase" there was an attempt to obscure the dramatic changes in policy, personnel, and allies, that distinguished the Morales from Velasco regimes. Fundamentally, these differences expressed a change in regime and not a simple shift in policy orientation to "consolidate the revolution," as the regime's propaganda argued.

Duros vs. Blandos

Although the national strike of 1977 accelerated the growing closeness between the military and traditional political actors and intensified efforts to define the transition schedule, it also opened up a new arena of conflict within the military. Differences in the military centered on the strategy and timing of the transition as well as the role of non-regime actors.[44] In Peru, the dispute between *duros* and *blandos* usually associated with the beginning of a transition process, was especially pronounced over how to respond to popular protests.

The success of the strike brought that issue to the forefront of the regime's agenda. Hard-liners, led by General Cisneros, favored a crackdown on leftist and union organizations, a prolonged and carefully con-

TABLE 2.2   Alliances of the Velasco and Morales Regimes

Velasco Regime (1968–1975)		*Morales Regime (1975–1980)*	
Allies	*Opponents*	*Allies*	*Opponents*
PC, CGTP,	APRA, AP, PPC	APRA, PPC[a]	PC,CGTP
New Corporate Organizations (SINAMOS, CNA, CONACI ...) MLR, OPRP	New Left, Business Sector, (CADE, SNI, CONACO)	Business Sector (CADE, SNI, CONACO)	New Left, Corporate Organizations (CNA, CONACI)
Prog. Church			Prog. Church

[a]Accion Popular abstained from participation in the Constituent Assembly elections.

trolled transition schedule (up to ten years), and a more explicit agreement with traditional parties, especially APRA. Favoring APRA was a calculated move against the political left. APRA was a party with a long history of union organization and was viewed as the only group that could contest the left's growing control of lower-class organizations.[45]

Ironically, where Velasco had favored the Communist Party to counteract the influence of APRA, the new regime looked to APRA with the hope of controlling the left. Unlike hard-liners, the *blandos* in the regime, including Morales himself, were reluctant to significantly increase repression against mobilized groups, fearing that would increase social conflict and threaten the entire process of extricating the military from direct political rule. Moreover, while favoring cooperation with APRA and other traditional groups, they were wary of developing the sort of political alliances that could threaten the predominance of the institutionalist position and once again "politicize" the military.

By the end of 1977 the national strike had strengthened the *blandos* in the regime. The strike had demonstrated that the regime would have to employ a higher level of repression if it was to reduce growing opposition to its rule. One month after the strike, the state of emergency was lifted and in October a decree was issued confirming the precise schedule of elections. The *duro* position suffered a further setback in May as a result of another national strike. The CGTP called this strike to protest a series of new economic measures, including price rises and wage freezes, and to demand the restitution of fired union leaders. The May 1978 strike was a forty-eight hour strike but was as successful as the twenty-four hour strike a year earlier. Even APRA adhered to this strike attempting to distance itself from the highly unpopular economic program being carried out. Street violence was more pronounced than in the July 1977 strike and repercussions of the strike were felt almost immediately in the regime. A cabinet reshuffle removed the most prominent hard-liners, replacing them with soft-line officials. The *blandos* consolidated their position in the regime with further cabinet changes in September, when the remaining hard-liners were ousted.[46]

By the inauguration of the Constituent Assembly, the military's internal conflicts over the transition process had been resolved. As with the removal of the progressive and *La Misión* officers, eliminating hard-liners from the regime underlined Morales' resolve to extract the military as rapidly as possible from direct political rule. This was clearly inspired by the "institutionalist" position that had resulted in the 1975 coup against General Velasco. Hard-liners favored committing the military to a set of explicit alliances with political actors and the prolongation of military rule—two goals diametrically opposed to the priorities of the institutionalist position. With the latter position now predominant in the regime, the acceleration of the transition process was assured.

Conclusion

The Velasco mobilization project was carried out from a state apparatus divided over the goals and methods of mobilization, handicapped by diminishing economic resources, and unable to effectively organize civil society. Without a prior consensus within the military on mobilization, the state became a battleground where different groups and interests carried out their policies. These groups, in alliance with a variety of organizations in society, confronted each other as well as those opposed to the entire scheme. Could things have worked out differently? While there is no doubt the regime suffered through some bad luck—Velasco's illness, fewer new oil discoveries than expected, a series of natural disasters such as the 1970 earthquake, and a shift in the El Niño current that crippled the fishing industry— it is difficult to see how a change in any of these events could have significantly altered the political outcome. Policy choices were limited by the overall philosophy of the "revolution." The military's ability to repress the New Left was hampered by the division within the regime over whether the New Left represented a serious threat and by the obvious contradiction this would have presented to a leadership that claimed to be a humanist-christian representative of the populace. Overall, given the conditions of state development in Peru, it is unlikely the outcome could have been significantly altered.

The transition from a situation of low state development, in which basic functions such as tax collection are carried out by a private firm, to an advanced state apparatus capable of overseeing the complex function of interest representation is a difficult one, especially in less than a decade. The 1975 coup against Velasco represented the first step in the dismantling of that project. The new regime proceeded to extricate the state from the task of political mobilization.

The increased conflicts provoked in the state and among its allies by the mobilization project, were a clear indication of the limits of state power in Peru. Another indication was the inability to translate the increased organization among popular sectors into a political identification with the state or an official party. If mobilization implies fundamental changes in behaviors and demands, then non-state actors were better able to respond to the new needs and demands of popular sectors than the state. In the race to mobilize among these sectors, the state, with its organizational and ideological difficulties, simply lost. Confronted by the vague and distant "humanist" identity offered by state organizations, or the identity offered by leftist unions and parties that linked their daily struggles with radical political demands, workers and peasants en masse opted for the latter. With the emergence of *clasista* organizations in the countryside and among the urban popular sectors, a new anti-system opposition began to develop. This would have serious implications for policy making in all three arenas of state power.

Notes

1. On the national security doctrine as developed in Brazil and the Southern Cone, see Genaro Arriagada, *El Pensamiento Político de los Militares: Estudios Sobre Chile, Argentina, Brasil y Uruguay* (Santiago: Centro de Investigaciones Socioeconomicos, n.d.).

2. Excellent analyses of these developments are found in Victor Villanueva, *Nueva Mentalidad Militar en el Perú?* (Lima: Ed. Mejía Baca, 1968) and *El CAEM y la Revolución de la Fuerza Armada* (Lima: Instituto de Estudios Peruanos, 1972). Also see Alfred Stepan, *State and Society: Peru in Comparative Perspective* (Princeton: Princeton University Press, 1978); Dirk Krujit *Revolución por Decreto* (Lima: Mosca Azul, 1990); and Daniel Masterson, *Militarism and Politics in Latin America: Peru From Sanchez Cerro to Sendero Luminoso* (Westport: Greenwood Press, 1991).

3. The Alianza Popular Revolucionaria Americana (APRA) was founded in Mexico City in 1924 by Victor Raúl Haya de la Torre. Until the mid-1950s the party followed a classic populist program and was effectively kept from power by military persecutions. After that point, APRA reached an accord with conservative leaders that shifted the party toward the right.

4. Interview with General Miguel Angel de la Flor in the collected interviews of Velasco era officers in María del Pilar Tello, *Golpe o Revolución?* (Lima: SAGSA, 1983), vol. 1, p. 43.

5. E.V.K. Fitzgerald, "State Capitalism in Peru," in Cynthia McClintock and Abraham Lowenthal, eds., *The Peruvian Experiment Reconsidered* (Princeton: Princeton University Press, 1983), p. 70.

6. On the agrarian reform, see José Matos Mar and José Manuel Mejía, *La Reforma Agraria en el Perú* (Lima: Instituto de Estudios Peruanos, 1980) and Cynthia McClintock, *Peasant Cooperatives and Political Change in Peru* (Princeton: Princeton University Press, 1981).

7. Susan Eckstein, "Revolution and Redistribution," in McClintock and Lowenthal, eds., *The Peruvian Experiment Reconsidered*, p. 347.

8. In his review of military literature in the period leading up to 1968, Stepan found virtually no mention of the mobilization problem. Stepan, *State and Society: Peru in Comparative Perspective*, p. 141. Moreover, none of the Velasco era generals interviewed by Del Pilar in 1983 suggested that the military had any mobilization plans prior to the 1968 coup. That was confirmed by this author in interviews with such officers during the 1987–1990 period.

9. Del Pilar Tello, vol. 2, p. 83.

10. David Scott Palmer, *Revolution from Above: Military Government and Popular Participation in Peru*, (Ithaca: Cornell University Dissertation Series, #47, 1973), p. 100.

11. SINAMOS pamphlets were widely distributed in shantytowns, factories, and the countryside. Their radical discourse included calls for the launching of "a militant struggle against the unjust social order," SINAMOS, "Características de la Revolución Peruana" (Lima: SINAMOS, n.d.).

12. General Jorge Fernández Maldonado, interview by author in Lima, September 1, 1987. Fernández Maldonado was one of the officers who most clearly emphasized the christian aspects of the regime's ideology, citing in particular the influence of liberation theology. On church-state relations in this period, see Jeffrey Klaiber, *La Iglesia en el Perú* (Lima: Pontificia Universidad Católica, 1988), pp. 375–407; and Luis Pásara, *Radicalización y Conflicto en la Iglesia Peruana* (Lima, El Virrey, 1987).

13. See *Marka*, May 1, 1975, p. 1 for a detailed history of events surrounding the formation of this group.

14. Henry Pease García, *El Ocaso del Poder Oligárquico* (Lima: DESCO, 1986), p. 148.

15. See General Leonidas Rodríguez's speech to workers in the SINAMOS pamphlet, "SINAMOS: Sindicalismo" (Lima: SINAMOS, 1972), p. 10. Rodríguez argues that "small partisan groups" have historically manipulated the labor movement. Also see Carlos Delgado, *El Proceso Revolucionario Peruano: Testimonio de Lucha* (Mexico DF: Siglo XXI, 1972).

16. A good example of this is Velasco's 1974 speech given on Independence Day (July 28th) and published as "La Participación en el Proceso Revolucionario," (Lima: Ediciones Juventud en Lucha, 1974).

17. For a fascinating account of the role of newspapers in this period see Guillermo Thorndike, *No, Mi General* (Lima: Mosca Azul, 1976).

18. Pease García, *El Ocaso del Poder Oligárquico*, pp. 114–121.

19. For example, Velasco was from a lower middle-class background in Piura, Rodríguez emerged from a working-class background in Cusco, and Tantaleán came from a family of small shopkeepers in Chota. A complete sociology of the Peruvian military has yet to be carried out.

20. See Denis Sulmont, *El Movimiento Obrero Peruano: 1890–1980,* 5th ed. (Lima: Ediciones Tareas, 1985).

21. Ministry of Labor figures reported in Giorgio Alberti, Jorge Santiestevan, and Luis Pásara, *Estado y Clase: La Comunidad Industrial en el Perú* (Lima: Instituto de Estudios Peruanos, 1977), p. 86.

22. Saturnino Paredes Macedo, *Los Sindicatos Clasistas y sus Principios* (Lima: CESEP, 1986), p. 66. The text sums up the most radical *clasista* tactic: "Apply through strikes the tactics of combat." Paredes was a founder of the Maoist Bandera Roja.

23. For an analysis of *clasismo* see especially Carmen Rosa Balbi, *Identidad Clasista en el Sindicalismo* (Lima: DESCO, 1989).

24. Sulmont, *El Movimiento Obrero*, p. 211.

25. Gustavo Espinoza, interview by author in Lima, July 9, 1988. Espinoza was secretary general of the CGTP during 1969–1976 and a member of the Communist Party's Central Committee.

26. CGTP, "Los Sindicatos y el Area Laboral de SINAMOS," (Lima: September 1972), p. 14.

27. The term "New Left" was used to describe the various groups that split away from the pro-Moscow Communist Party during the 1960s. Divided into nearly twenty separate groups, most were organized clandestinely among students and popular sectors. A detailed discussion of this phenomenon is found in Ricardo Letts, *La Izquierda Peruana* (Lima: Mosca Azul, 1981); Enrique Bernales, *Socialismo y Nacion* (Lima: Mesa Redonda, 1987); Guillermo Rochabrun, "Izquierda, Democracia y Crisis en el Perú," *Margenes* 3, 1989, pp. 79–99.

28. Comité de Coordinación y Unificación Sindical Clasista (CUSCC): II Asamblea Nacional Sindical Clasista, "Conclusiones y Resoluciones," (Lima: CCUSC, 1976), pp. 2–4.

29. SINAMOS, "El Fenomeno Ultra," (Lima: SINAMOS, n.d.), p. 10. This document was part of a series of evaluations done by SINAMOS on the different political forces in the country.

30. Sulmont, *El Movimiento Obrero Peruano,* pp. 198–201.

31. Aldo Panfichi, "La Crisis y las Multitudes: Lima, 5 de Febrero de 1975," *Debates en Sociología* 9, 1983, pp. 31–64.

32. Comité Ejecutivo Nacional, "Comunicado del Partido Aprista Peruano sobre los Sucesos del 5 de Febrero," (Lima: APRA, 1975).

33. *Marka*, May 1, 1975, p. 17.

34. *Marka*, May 1, 1975, p. 2, reports of several meetings among top military commanders on the issue of succession.

35. *Marka*, July 12, 1975, p. 5.

36. These views were expressed to the author by General Francisco Morales Bermúdez in an interview, June 20, 1988.

37. Personal interviews with two members of *La Orga*, May 20, 1988, and May 31, 1988. Also see Raúl Gonzales, "MRTA: La Historia Desconocida," *QueHacer* 51, 1988, p. 33. Gonzales makes a connection between *La Orga* and the later guerrilla group, MRTA.

38. Diego García Sayan, *Las Tomas de Tierras en el Perú* (Lima: DESCO, 1982), p. 197. The literature on the CCP and this peasant movement is abundant, although few U.S. scholars have studied the theme. See Rodrigo Sánchez, *Tomas de Tierras y Conciencia Política Campesina* (Lima: Instituto de Estudios Peruanos, 1982). Also see the personal testimony of Andahuaylas peasant leader Lino Quintanilla, *Andahuaylas: La Lucha por la Tierra* (Lima: Mosca Azul, 1981); and Confederación Campesina del Perú, "Plataforma de Lucha," (Lima: CCP 1974).

39. Drago Kisic, *De la Corresponsabilidad a la Moratoria: El Caso de la Deuda Peruana, 1970–1986* (Lima: Fundación Friedrich Ebert, 1987).

40. Letts, *La Izquierda Peruana,* p. 68.

41. An analysis of the positions taken by leftist parties during this period is found in Jorge Nieto, *Izquierda y Democracia en el Perú: 1975–1980* (Lima: DESCO, 1983). For a comparative perspective on the transition see Guillermo O'Donnell,

Philippe Schmitter, and Laurence Whitehead, *Transitions from Authoritarian Rule: Tentative Conclusions on Uncertain Outcomes* (Baltimore: Johns Hopkins University Press, 1985).

42. "Plan de Gobierno Tupac Amaru," *Ultima Hora*, October 10, 1977, p. 14.

43. Henry Pease García, *Los Caminos del Poder* (Lima: DESCO, 1981), pp. 204–206.

44. The general scheme and definition of *duros* and *blandos* is discussed in O'Donnell, Schmitter, and Whitehead, eds., *Transitions from Authoritarian Rule*, p. 15.

45. These points were made by General Luis Cisneros Vizquerra, interview by author in Lima, August 28, 1988.

46. On the May 1978 strike, see CGTP, "Mayo 22–23: Testimonio de la CGTP," (Lima: CGTP, 1978); and CGTP, "Documentos: V Congreso," (Lima: CGTP, 1978).

3

International Actors
and the Politics of Economic Austerity

As Peru entered the late 1970s, it faced a major economic downturn and rising social conflict. Neoliberalism, which emphasizes minimal state regulation of the economy and prioritizes market-oriented adjustments over distributive policies, guided economic policy making from 1978 to 1984. To a large extent, these policies responded to significant external pressures brought on by Peru's growing foreign debt. The inability to meet debt obligations led to a significant loss of state control over the economy to international actors, especially to the International Monetary Fund (IMF). This chapter will analyze the interplay between these economic and political factors and how they affected state power.

First, the role of international lending agencies and neoliberal policies is examined; second, the impact of these policies on state capacities is evaluated. The restrictions on state decision making inherent in the IMF prescriptions were compounded by specific policies adopted by the Morales and Belaúnde governments to reduce the size and capacities of the state. Both governments reduced state resources in ways that impeded, restricted, or curtailed bureaucratic capacities. Neoliberal attacks on the state were carried out with strong political criteria that often led to new inefficiencies rather than the promised streamlining. The neoliberal offensive against the regulatory role of the state was accompanied by an attack on many of the new rights gained by popular sector organizations during the Velasco period.

Finally, I examine the conflicts that resulted from the implementation of neoliberal policies and the responses of the state. Among popular sectors, protest occurred not only in the streets but at the ballot box. Leftist parties won an unexpectedly large vote in 1978 in protest against Morales. This was repeated when the new electoral coalition United Left

(IU) swept the 1983 municipal elections. The economic crisis also opened the way for the formation of new popular sector organizations to meet the needs of the poor.

The challenges faced by the Peruvian state from 1978 to 1985 from international financial institutions, newly mobilized popular sectors, and ineffective policy making were compounded by the country's economic recession. As resources declined, state companies became decapitalized, tax revenues shrank, and deficits shot up. The state was, thus, in a far more vulnerable economic position in the mid-1980s than it had been before, and developments in the latter part of that decade only further exacerbated this situation.

The Pressure to Adjust and the Transition

Between 1977 and 1979, Peru went through a period of IMF-directed orthodox adjustment. The causes of the crisis were varied and have been analyzed elsewhere.[1] They included a sharp drop in the price of Peru's traditional mineral exports due to the world recession, the lack of new petroleum reserves upon which most government planners had based their economic forecasts, a decline in domestic and foreign private investment in the face of growing social and political unrest, increased deficits in the public sector resulting from nationalizations, and rising inflation and balance of payments problems.

Morales' attempt to implement austerity programs, beginning soon after the 1975 coup, failed to resolve the economic problems facing the country and accentuated social conflicts. The initial austerity program was carried out with an agreement between the Morales regime and the private banks. The banks, led by New York's Citibank and including Chase Manhattan, Morgan Guaranty, and Wells Fargo, agreed to lend Peru $400 million in exchange for an orthodox stabilization program and policies that would favor foreign investment, such as a resolution of outstanding disputes for nationalized companies. As Stallings notes, "Not since the 1920s had private banks become so involved in the domestic affairs of a foreign government."[2]

By 1977, with few signs of a recovery or progress on resolving balance of payments difficulties, Peru was forced to look for more foreign financing (see Table 3.1). What occurred next underlined the new power of international finance in directing the Peruvian economy. Under pressure from private banks, who refused to offer new loans without an IMF agreement, Peru signed a letter of intent with the IMF that included the latter's strict supervision over the economy. However, the agreement broke down less than six months after the IMF concluded targets were not being met. After all foreign financing, including U.S. aid, came to a

TABLE 3.1   External Public Debt (in millions of dollars), 1970–1985

Year	External Public Debt	Debt Service	Debt Service As % of GNP	Debt Service As % of Exports
1970	911	173	2.7	16.7
1971	918	215	3.0	24.2
1972	1,121	219	2.4	23.2
1973	1,491	433	4.0	38.9
1974	2,182	456	3.4	30.3
1975	3,036	474	2.9	35.6
1976	3,554	485	3.1	36.2
1977	4,311	622	4.4	36.0
1978	5,135	929	7.6	47.1
1979	5,764	1,364	8.8	37.1
1980	6,043	1,695	6.5	43.3
1981	6,210	1,836	7.2	56.5
1982	6,908	1,600	6.2	48.6
1983	8,339	1,791	9.0	59.4
1984	9,731	2,331	11.1	74.1
1985	10,510	2,067	11.5	69.4

Source: Adapted from "Balanza de Pagos," *Actualidad Economica* 11, July 1987, p. 21.

screeching halt as a result of the IMF decision, a new agreement was reached. The regime clearly had little leverage in its negotiations with the IMF, given its need to refinance its loans and maintain access to international credit. The pressures to resist IMF austerity measures came primarily from the popular sectors and from some groups in the military who saw many of their perks threatened, including arms purchases. Nonetheless, the Peruvian state was highly dependent on foreign financing and would have faced possible collapse without it. The choice of ceding some state decision-making authority was not a palatable one but was made because there were no other serious options.

The influence of international financial institutions over a Third World state during economic adjustments is quite high, yet very specific.[3] It tends to be stronger during the initial decision-making stages and less so during the implementation of policies. Moreover, international actors have greater influence with the small group of policy officials in a minis-try or presidential palace than with the lower-level bureaucrats and local officials who will actually carry out policies and are more sensitive to opposition. It is not surprising, therefore, that the agreement between Peru and the IMF broke down during the implementation stage. The type of pressure exercised by international economic actors may also vary. Stallings describes three mechanisms of international economic influence: markets, linkage and leverage.[4] Peru in this period felt pressure from all of these mechanisms.

With the prices of exports low in international markets until late 1978, Peru was forced to borrow and remain vulnerable to interest rate pres-sures in the financial markets. The leverage of international actors, including banks and the IMF, was also high, given the large debt Peru was forced to service, the scarcity of resources, and the unity of creditors. That leverage was made known by the cut off of international aid and the conditioning of new funds on an agreement with the IMF. Finally, the linkage between policy makers in Peru and the international financial community was very strong and gave international actors a privileged position within the decision-making circles of both the Morales and Belaúnde governments. When the Morales regime adopted adjustment policies it also turned toward business leaders and technocrats with inter-national connections, such as Walter Piazza, Javier Silva Ruete, and Manuel Moreyra, to develop its economic policies.

Despite the various and haphazard austerity packages adopted between 1975 and 1978, public expenditures and the government deficit continued to rise. To a large extent, this reflected the growing importance of debt payments as a percentage of government expenditures. In addi-tion, while government wages and investment in public enterprises declined, military spending increased significantly. As the 100th anniver-sary of the War of the Pacific approached, border tensions mounted with neighboring Chile, where General Augusto Pinochet had vastly increased the power and size of the Chilean armed forces. The Peruvian armed forces initiated a veritable buying spree in the mid-70s by spending between 25 and 40 percent of the budget on arms purchases and contract-ing new debt obligations.[5]

With the problem of public sector deficits left largely unresolved, Peru entered an economic recovery in late 1978 (see Table 3.2). It's GNP grew over 3 percent for the first time in four years, while exports increased over 78 percent from the previous year.[6] As Wise and others have argued, the turnaround in the economy had less to do with the austerity of previous years than with the revival of prices for Peru's petroleum and mineral exports. As the economy improved, Morales and the new civilian president began renewed foreign borrowing, setting the stage for the next round of IMF directed austerity.

Peru's external vulnerabilities involved more than the IMF's role in directing austerity. Continued dependence on primary product exports made the economy highly susceptible to fluctuations in international prices and demonstrated how state power was contingent upon the international market. The increased resources needed to cover growing deficits came from a favorable, but temporary, turn in international market forces--the same forces that had brought on the 1974–1978 crisis.

Neoliberalism and the State

The implementation of a neoliberal state reform program has a number of possible pitfalls. When introducing privatizations and adjustment policies, the state, which in neoliberal theory is the source of the disequilibriums affecting an economy, is ironically entrusted to be part of the solution.[7] As a result, a state apparatus with low capacities in all arenas of state power may find it difficult to effectively implement adjustment programs. A haphazard effort to reduce the size and role of the state where state capacities are already limited, runs the risk of creating more inefficiencies by sacrificing valuable organizational resources. This is precisely what happened in Peru in the early 1980s. It was an error that later neoliberal reformers under President Fujimori avoided by simulta-

TABLE 3.2   Public Sector Deficits and GNP Growth, 1970–1985

Year	GNP Growth[a]	Gvt. Deficit[b]	Year	GNP Growth[a]	Gvt. Deficit[b]
1970	5.9	1.2	1978	0.3	4.5
1971	4.2	2.6	1979	5.8	0.5
1972	2.9	3.1	1980	4.5	2.4
1973	5.4	3.4	1981	4.4	3.9
1974	9.2	2.7	1982	0.3	3.1
1975	3.4	4.6	1983	−12.3	7.2
1976	2.0	5.5	1984	4.8	4.0
1977	0.4	6.6	1985	2.5	2.1

[a] Percentage change over previous year.
[b] Public Sector Deficit as a percent of GNP.

Source: Instituto Nacional de Estadistica, *Compendio Estadistico*, 1986 (Lima: INE, 1987), pp. 79, 205.

neously liberalizing the economy and strengthening essential state capacities.

The effort to reduce the state's role in the economy did not fully begin until the 1980 inauguration of the civilian Belaúnde administration. The continuities between the Morales and Belaúnde regimes became apparent when Belaúnde announced the formation of his cabinet and economic team. In his inaugural speech, Prime Minister Manuel Ulloa confirmed that the new regime would continue the stabilization policies implemented by its authoritarian predecessor. The Ulloa priorities were similar to those of Morales' former finance minister Javier Silva Ruete: reducing import restrictions and cutting state subsidies, in particular price subsidies. The Ulloa stabilization policy also encouraged greater foreign investment, especially in the increasingly important petroleum sector.[8] The key difference between the two orientations was that the Belaúnde administration emphasized reducing the state's role in the economy. Plans were developed to sell shares in a variety of state companies, including the national airline, with incentives to private investors. Moreover, regulations governing banks and the financial sector were significantly liberalized. By the end of 1981 the government produced a list of eighty "sellable" state-owned companies to be sold to the private sector.[9] The neoliberal offensive also attempted to alter the cooperative schemes introduced by the Velasco regime. In late 1980, the AP majority and its PPC allies in congress voted to give Belaúnde special legislative powers to revise the various military decrees issued during the previous twelve years.

Armed with those new powers, the executive tightened the regulations governing agrarian cooperatives and downgraded the "social property" sector. In addition, a new law introduced in early 1981 decreed that the shares of a company belonging to "labor communities" could be freely exchanged, thus allowing companies to buy back these shares and reduce worker influence. Nonetheless, the effort to eliminate labor communities completely fell apart when a government poll designed to decide the final fate of this experiment resulted in overwhelming worker support for the existing scheme.[10] Aside from changing the rules over the cooperative sector, the regime could do little to reverse the important legacies of Velasco that the neoliberal economic advisors of Belaúnde objected the most to: the agrarian reform, *estabilidad laboral*, the near monopoly of state companies in "strategic" sectors of the economy, and the left's control of the labor and peasant movements.

Both the agrarian reform and *estabilidad laboral* were part of the new constitution that would have been politically risky to alter so soon after its inauguration. Aside from minor tinkering, Belaúnde left those reforms intact. On the other hand, some state-controlled companies were sold, but these were mostly small firms and not the large state enterprises such as PetroPerú. The sale of these large "strategic" companies would have been impractical, especially given the lack of buyers. Beyond these practical reasons, the lack of consensus within the Belaúnde administration on how far to pursue neoliberal objectives also limited this approach.[11] Party officials complained of their low influence in the administration and of a monopoly on decision making by neoliberal technocrats linked to Ulloa. It would be nearly a decade before a new neoliberal offensive overcame some of the more structural obstacles impeding this agenda.

Despite these limitations, Belaúnde's policies represented the culmination of an attack on state economic prerogatives begun in the mid-1970s. The effects on state policy-making capabilities were severe, especially for public sector employees. Under both Morales and Belaúnde, public sector wages were cut significantly and large numbers of experienced workers were forced to resign. At some ministries, up to 70 percent of the work force was eliminated. The majority of dismissed employees had over five years of job experience.[12] The public sector clearly lost a pool of experienced personnel and, as it became an insecure and unrewarded sector of employment, it also lost the ability to again attract highly qualified expertise.

In a similar vein, the sale of state enterprises rather than resulting in streamlining usually provided greater leeway for the use of clientelism, corruption, and waste of resources. This was especially true during the Belaúnde administration, where family and party ties served as litmus tests for high level appointments. Politically connected private investors sought favorable laws that would give them special access or priority to newly sold companies or allow the sale of state assets at bargain basement prices. An immediate outcome of such political favoritism was an increase in corruption scandals. The collapse of the banking sector in mid-1983, when three major banks declared bankruptcy, was partly a result of wheeling and dealing by well-connected and, thus, politically immune bankers.[13]

Corruption and clientelism were not the only problems fostered by the reckless application of neoliberal policies under Belaúnde. Faced with a number of state companies that were to be sold but had no buyers, the government pursued a strategy of weakening the firms by eliminating investments or encouraging the entry of foreign competitors. The two most notable examples were in PescaPerú, where two-thirds of the workforce was eliminated and the once buoyant fishing fleet was put in dry dock, and SiderPerú, which was virtually shut down because government actions permitted foreign "dumping" of steel.[14] These sorts of kamikaze attacks on the state sector were justified as eliminating an unnecessary drag on the state's finances. Yet the practice clearly wasted state resources that could have been more rationally eliminated or redirected.

Moreover, the neoliberal approach to macroeconomic management significantly weakened the state's position internationally. The revival of international prices for Peru's traditional mineral exports during 1978 and 1979 was seen as solving the economic crisis, although it did not address the underlying problems of the economy. Accompanying this laissez-faire approach was trade liberalization that brought down tariff barriers and ended a series of subsidies and favorable terms for domestic industrialists. Although the Belaúnde administration reversed itself under intense business pressure, the overall approach to economic management relied on the continued boom in traditional exports. Along with this came foreign borrowing to support Peru's arms build-up and to implement Belaúnde's expensive road building projects in the Amazonian region. By 1982 the international economic cycle turned against Peru's interests when mineral prices declined sharply and interest rates rose. The prices of Peru's mineral exports fell on international markets, while both the agricultural and fishing sectors felt the adverse effects of climatic changes caused by the Pacific current "El Niño."

The Belaunde administration's lowering of import restrictions significantly hurt Peru's weak manufacturing industry and led to an 11.5 percent decline in 1983 alone. The crisis affected all sectors of Peru's economy. The GNP, which had grown by 4.5 percent in 1980 and had declined to .3 percent growth in 1982, experienced a negative growth rate of 12.3 percent in 1983, one of the worst declines since the War of the Pacific. To find new funds to avoid a further collapse, the administration turned to foreign banks and lending agencies. The result was a dramatic increase in Peru's foreign debt. In 1984, 74 percent of the country's export income was dedicated to servicing the debt (see Table 3.1).

The debt crisis of 1983–1985 compounded the economic difficulties confronting the Belaúnde regime and demonstrated the serious political and economic limits of the neoliberal policies of Morales and Belaúnde. As the economy entered a recession, it became politically untenable to continue to submit the country to IMF-imposed austerity and debt servicing that ate up most of Peru's export earnings. The foreign debt raised the specter of a state which had completely lost its ability to direct and influence the flow of economic resources. The crisis clearly illustrated that the country's myriad problems had not been solved by austerity packages and the traditional export boom. Peru's reliance on a liberal export-oriented model and its heavy external borrowing left the state more exposed than ever to pressure by international actors.

From 1981 to 1984, Belaúnde increased the foreign debt to deal with the problems of recession and declining exports. The new minister of economy, Carlos Rodríguez Pastor, a former official of the Wells Fargo Bank, negotiated new loans for the country. In return he committed the regime to further austerity measures, including sharp rises in gasoline prices and cuts in public spending. Within a year, however, the IMF austerity agreement collapsed after it was discovered that accounting tricks were disguising Peru's inability to meet economic targets. After another brief IMF agreement in 1984 also collapsed, the Belaúnde administration admitted it could not meet quarterly targets and Peru effectively put a moratorium on debt payments.

The de facto moratorium came after nearly a decade of IMF- directed austerity and with the government facing rising social protest at home. Opposition candidates for the upcoming 1985 presidential elections attacked the government for its willingness to cede to foreign banks, and public opinion turned sharply against continuing timely payments of debt obligations. Both opponents and members of the cabinet argued that payment of the debt restricted the prospects of future growth by exporting badly needed capital that could be reinvested in the country. The president of the Central Bank, Richard Webb, argued like many that new terms should be negotiated with creditors, while others, including presidential hopeful Alan García, supported a unilateral restriction of payments.

The debt crisis of the early 1980s illustrates the links between domestic and international arenas of state power. In Peru's precarious economic situation, few resources were left to distribute and planning took a back seat to satisfying the demands of international creditors. The administrative capacity of the state declined and the ability of the state to provide social services or support for key social sectors was also curtailed. For underdeveloped countries, the option of not meeting debt obligations usually resulted in estrangement from the international economic system, something an economy dependent on the export of traditional products such as Peru's could ill afford (see Table 3.3). Yet international lenders, including the IMF and the industrial countries, were generally unsympathetic to the social costs of austerity and had no mechanisms to compensate for the drain on badly needed economic resources. The debt moratorium, and later García's more radical continuation of that policy, were desperate responses to avert the possibility of economic and social collapse.

Economic Austerity and Social Conflict

The austerity and adjustment policies implemented in the decade from the overthrow of Velasco until the election of Alan García (1975–85) significantly increased the level of social conflict in Peru by contributing to a series of general strikes and other labor, peasant, and squatter pro-

TABLE 3.3   Principal Exports (in millions of dollars), 1977–1985

Products	1977	1978	1979	1980	1981	1982	1983	1984	1985
Fishmeal	184	196	258	195	141	202	80	137	118
Agriculture[a]	324	253	328	225	170[c]	219	195	198	225
Minerals[b]	906	936	1517	1795	1493	1312	1578	1368	1207
Petroleum	52	186	652	792	690	719	544	618	645
OtherTraditional	36	48	113	84	54	79	63	100	71
Total Traditional	1502	1619	2866	3071	2548	2531	2460	2421	2264
Total Non-Traditional	224	353	810	845	701	762	555	726	714

[a] Agricultural exports include cotton, sugar, and coffee.
[b] Mineral exports included are copper, iron, gold, silver, lead, and zinc.
[c] Figure for sugar not included.

Source: Authors elaboration from Richard Webb and Graciela Fernández-Baca, *Peru en Numeros* (Lima: Cuanto SA: 1991), pp. 922–23.

tests, over their worsening standard of living. Protests took place on the streets, in factories and universities, and at the ballot boxes. The implementation of neoliberal policies coincided with the return to civilian rule and, thus, provided newly enfranchised sectors an additional outlet to express their frustration. The political left was the main beneficiary of popular sector frustration. It consolidated its political position and remained the principal organizer of the lower-class. However, these sectors also demonstrated strong self-organization at the local and neighborhood levels to confront the economic crisis on a daily basis. These independent self-help organizations were one of the most important legacies of the crisis.

The first indication of the political impact of austerity came with the 1978 election of a constituent assembly to draw up a new constitution. The timing of the election could not have been worse for the Morales regime. It came only one month after the second successful general strike and four days after a new economic "package" of price rises was announced. With Peru's GNP falling sharply, including negative growth rates in 1977 and 1978, the impact on Peru's popular sector was especially dramatic. Unemployment rose from 4.2 percent in 1973 to 7.0 percent in 1978 (underemployment rose to over 50 percent). Wages were reduced by nearly one-half, while the cost of living quintupled between 1973 and

1979.[15] The level of social conflict was at a peak and included anti-regime campaigns conducted by competing parties. The left aimed its campaign at the lower-class, attacking the Morales austerity measures. Of Peru's parties, only APRA decided not to run on an anti-military platform, arguing that the campaign should be focused on the design of the new constitution.[16]

The election results were a surprise to most observers. As expected, APRA received the largest share (35%) of the votes. However, the five leftist parties that presented candidates unexpectedly won a third of the vote. Prior to the elections, over twenty leftist parties consolidated their forces to five parties.[17] These parties were given little chance of receiving a significant share of the vote, given their inexperience in electoral politics and, aside from the Communist Party, a low recognition of their symbols. However, one factor working in their favor was the name recognition of most of their candidates. Almost all of the left's candidates had been active in popular sector organizations during the previous decade and were known as vehement opponents of the military regime. Voting for the left was, therefore, a plebiscitarian rejection of the regime.

After the elections, the two traditional parties garnering the most votes, APRA and the PPC, reached a power-sharing agreement that guaranteed them control of the assembly. Assembly leadership was given to the aging leader of APRA, Victor Raúl Haya de la Torre. Leftist assembly members were not assigned important positions in the assembly and did not take part in most of the deliberations. This was partly by choice. For many on the left, the assembly was only one "arena" of the political struggle against the regime and served to promote the demands of popular sectors.[18] The anti-system nature of the opposition meant that their participation in the elections and the assembly was not to support and consolidate the processes and institutions of the transition, but rather to "create a leftist current in the country" and "advance and support popular struggles."[19] Unlike the majority parties, leftist members did not view writing the constitution as the most significant task for the assembly. Ultimately, the left opposed the thrust of the document that was written and refused to sign the final version.

For many leftist assembly members, such as Javier Diez Canseco and Carlos Malpica, participating in street protests, rallies, and hunger strikes, was more important than writing the constitution. In the assembly, leftist opposition leaders denounced the APRA-PPC majority and the military regime. These shared opposition activities increased cooperation between groups on the left that had been competitors throughout most of the decade.

Despite the return to civilian rule in 1980 and the short-lived economic recovery of 1979–1982, the level of social conflict remained high.

Popular sector organizations were openly hostile to policies they held responsible for their declining incomes and rising unemployment. This hostility was compounded by governments that did little to reach out to these organizations and, in fact, considered them enemies. Belaunde's Acción Popular had no significant organization among these sectors and the new civilian government, content with its wide margins of victory in the elections, had no plans to develop such organizations. Belaúnde thus conceded the organizational monopoly of the left among the lower-classes while he attacked leftist organizations for being "unrepresenta-tive" of these sectors. The result was an antagonistic and hostile relation-ship between popular sector organizations and the regime.

Faced with a new wave of protests and strikes in 1981 and with its own limited influence on these sectors, the Belaúnde administration opted for a new scheme designed to reduce social conflict and reach policy consensus. The result was the Comisión Nacional Tripartita (CNT) composed of representatives from business (CONFIEP, SNI); labor (CGTP, CTP, and what remained of the CTRP); and the ministries of labor and economy. It was to address labor demands (e.g. restitution of fired labor leaders) and to coordinate wage and price rises with its members through a process of consensus and specific accords. If the process of *con-certación* succeeded, the system was to be expanded to other policy areas, such as housing and agriculture.

The CNT was formed in the hopes of satisfying the demands of unions and reducing the growing number of strikes. The first two years of the Belaúnde government witnessed a 50 percent increase in the number of strikes. The immediate aim of this new wave of strike activity was to reverse the dramatic fall in wages that had occurred since the mid-1970s, a goal which was only partially achieved.[20]

Soon after the CNT's formation a tentative accord was reached on prices and wages: all members agreed that salaries should be increased to offset the rising cost of living. This point was especially crucial to labor insofar as salaries had deteriorated substantially in the previous seven years and inflation was on the rise (a record 70 percent in 1981). In addi-tion, the accord stipulated that price rises should occur within the limits to be negotiated between the government and individual sectors in sepa-rate commissions.[21] Barely six months after this accord, however, it became apparent that the goals would be virtually impossible to accom-plish. Inflation increased beyond government estimates and most busi-nesses balked at the notion of effectively indexing wages. With no mechanisms to enforce the agreements and with infighting in the Belaúnde cabinet over economic policy raging, the CNT was reduced to little more than informal meetings to air grievances. By mid-1982 the

CGTP withdrew its participation, arguing that neither the government nor business had adhered to the accord.

The Belaúnde administration's inability to reduce social tensions or significantly ameliorate the living conditions of the popular sectors led to growing polarization. This was most evident in the 1983 municipal elections. With APRA distracted and divided by a power struggle to succeed the recently deceased party chief, Victor Raúl Haya de la Torre, the most sustained and sharpest attacks on government policy came from the newly formed coalition of leftist parties, the United Left (IU). Their criticism centered on the regime's economic policies, especially the deterioration of salaries and the growing openness to international corporations. By early 1983, the increasing difficulties confronting the government helped consolidate the IU as the main opposition to the AP-PPC regime.

Electoral opposition was not the only form of protest challenging regime policies. The increased activity of the Maoist Sendero Luminoso added to the growing exhaustion of the Belaúnde government. Sendero had a strong base in provincial universities and was Peru's only regional leftist party. This regionalism isolated the party during the 1970s mobilization process. Sendero launched its military offensive in 1980 on the day that presidential elections were held, bent on carrying out a Maoist revolutionary project "from the countryside to the cities." Over the next two years, most of its armed activity was restricted to Ayacucho and the surrounding area. In 1983, Sendero significantly stepped up its activity, launching its first major offensive in Lima. Apparently unable to halt the increasing violence, Belaúnde also came under attack for the growing human rights violations committed by the armed forces in Ayacucho.[22] In the face of such attacks, the government accused critics of being linked to subversion and a worldwide campaign against Peru's image.

Against this background of political exhaustion, the 1983 municipal elections were held. Those elections soon turned into a mid-term referendum on the regime, similar to the 1978 constituent assembly elections for the Morales regime. The elections also helped consolidate IU's position as the main opposition to the regime. As one IU leader noted, IU's campaign emphasized the elections as a "plebiscitarian process where the people should decide to reject the maintenance of the government's economic policy."[23] In Lima both AP and APRA presented weak candidates, leaving the field open for IU and the PPC. Under these conditions, IU did well (see Table 3.4). Not only did IU's Alfonso Barrantes win the municipality of Lima, but IU candidates won most of the major municipalities of the southern and central parts of the country: Tacna, Puno, Cusco, Arequipa, Huancayo, and Huaraz. APRA swept its traditional strongholds in the north such as Trujillo and Cajamarca. By contrast, the loss for AP and the

PPC was significant as both parties failed to win any major city outside of the Amazonian region. Nationwide, AP only captured 17 percent of the vote, while the PPC fared even worse with 14 percent of the total vote.

IU candidates received the greatest number of votes from the "marginal" districts of Lima where working class and shantytown areas now represented nearly half the Lima electorate. The 1983 elections demonstrated the electoral importance of these districts and the growing link between IU and the urban lower-class. As the political base of IU, lower-class districts received priority attention from the new municipal government. The newly elected Mayor of Lima, Alfonso Barrantes, and local IU-controlled districts undertook the first sustained effort since the Velasco regime at promoting popular mobilization. One of the most interesting experiments were the new social welfare programs based on models of *autogestion* or self-government, also adopted during the Velasco era. The emphasis in these programs was on local neighborhood decision making with no official role for governmental organs. As we shall see in the chapter on Villa El Salvador, this arrangement provided a base for anti-system opposition to flourish and also effectively limited the ability of the state to implement many of its policies.

In early 1984 the municipality of Lima initiated the "Glass of Milk Program," to guarantee all children one glass of milk per day.[24] With the assistance of non-governmental organizations (NGOs), international agencies, and church groups, the program set up a vast distribution network involving the formation of committees of glasses of milk (comités de vaso de leche, CVL) in each marginal district and CVL zones within those districts. At the same time, "popular kitchen" programs were introduced, allowing a group of residents to buy food in quantity

TABLE 3.4   Presidential Election Results, 1978–1985 (percentage of total vote)

Party	1978	1980	1983	1985
AP	–	45.4	17.4	7.6
PPC	23.8	9.6	13.8	11.9
APRA	35.3	27.4	33.0	53.1
Left (Total)[a]	29.4	13.9	28.8	24.7

[a] Left vote for 1978 elections includes PRT, UNIR, UI, UDP, FOCEP, PSR, PCP. 1980–1985 vote corresponds to United Left (IU).

Source: Fernando Tuesta Soldevilla, *Perú Político en Cifras* (Lima: Friedrich Ebert, 1987), pp. 197, 205, 221, 229.

and cook low-cost meals within a neighborhood. These programs had originally developed during the 1970s as a way to lower food costs for people in a shantytown. Each member had to participate and contribute equally in the costs and preparation of meals. The first popular kitchens emerged in the late 1970s and were initiated by neighborhood church groups and clubs. By 1983 a network of kitchens was already operating at the district level, sharing experiences and providing technical assistance to other groups. The experience of the *"Independiente"* kitchen in the district of El Agustino is perhaps typical:

> It was organized by the Mothers' Club 'Nuestra Señora del Carmen' which had been reorganized in March 1981. During nine months we worked to collect funds, receiving help from the 'Coordinación de Comedores de El Agustino' with the donation of 2 kitchens and food from CARITAS. We also received advice from the parish and the organizational experience of other kitchens.[25]

In both the CVL and popular kitchens, the participants were mostly women who were members of local mother's clubs and neighborhood associations. Their organization was based on *autogestión*: members actively participated in preparing and distributing food and, most importantly, leaders were elected on a regular basis. In the case of the CVLs,

> Generally the women are local neighborhood leaders in charge of social assistance. They were elected in democratic assemblies as coordinators of the program. These coordinators, along with the treasurer and those responsible for health and food control, constitute the nucleus of the directive of a Committee of Glass of Milk, defining the criteria and norms used in the preparation and distribution of resources.[26]

By the end of 1988 there were 7,458 CVLs and 643 popular kitchens in Lima alone.[27] The growth of these groups, in addition to the promotion of "popular libraries" and "health committees," indicated the ongoing mobilization of popular sectors in Lima's marginal districts. In the 1970s, the poor were mobilized around such issues as access to electricity and schools. The new mobilization issues were food and health, which reflected how severely the popular sectors had suffered from the prolonged economic crisis.

In both the CVL and popular kitchens, the local neighborhood character of the organization, the election of local leaders, as well as the multiple and decentralized norms governing distribution, reduced the ability of traditional state actors to impose their norms. These same factors inhibited any one political actor from becoming the predominant clientelist agent. Diverse groups, including the different parties of IU, the Catholic

Church, and NGOs, played an active role in the organizational process and the relationships which developed usually depended on peculiarly local circumstances.[28]

Moreover, the political moment appeared to favor implementing these schemes with a minimum of state interference. The Belaúnde administration was more concerned with the crumbling economy, increased terrorism, and political infighting within the governing AP-PPC coalition, than with the possible effects of the opposition's participationist experiments. In addition, IU-controlled municipalities attempted to demonstrate the efficacy of the model of *autogestión* with a minimum of control "from above" in order to consolidate its lower-class base.

Conclusion

The economic crises which plagued Peru from the mid-1970s through the early 1980s significantly weakened both state organizational capabilities and leverage in the international arena. To some extent, this weakening seemed self-inflicted, as with Belaúnde's approach to state enterprise management or his administration's reliance on external borrowing and a short-lived export boom. Yet much of the weakening resulted from structural factors beyond any policy makers control, particularly the international environment that was highly unfavorable to Peru. The IMF, which played a crucial role in Peru during this period, did not place a high value on the "social costs" to Peru as a result of its austerity program. On the other hand, Peru had little influence on its international creditors to improve its payment conditions or lessen the pain of austerity. The direction the IMF led Peru's economy during 1977–78 indicated the state's loss of control over resource management to an outside actor.

A key factor influencing decision making in this period was social conflict from newly mobilized sectors. The popular sector exerted pressure through its protests and strikes and forced the Morales and Belaúnde regimes to backtrack on previously announced policies which created a high degree of uncertainty for decision makers. The attempt at policy *concertación* demonstrated an interest in limiting social conflict, yet its failure exposed the state to increased difficulties in implementing policies in the face of protests. The neoliberal orientation that guided state policy tended to strengthen the political identification of the popular sectors with the left and its anti-system discourse. Economic austerity "packages" introduced by Morales and Belaúnde had a negative effect on lower-class incomes and strengthened the left's monopoly on lower-class organization developed under Velasco. These sectors increasingly took their protests from the streets, universities, and meeting halls, into the ballot boxes.

Notes

1. Among the most important works in this area are Barbara Stallings, "International Capitalism and the Peruvian Military Government: 1968–1978," in Cynthia McClintock and Abraham Lowenthal, eds., *The Peruvian Experiment Reconsidered* (Princeton: Princeton University Press, 1983), pp. 144–180; Rosemary Thorp and Geoffrey Bertram, *Peru 1890–1977: Growth and Policy in an Open Economy* (New York: Columbia University Press, 1978); Felipe Portocarrero, *Crisis y Recuperación* (Lima: Mosca Azul, 1980); and Daniel Schlydowsky and Juan Wicht, *Anatomía de un Fracaso Económico: Perú, 1968–1978* (Lima: CIUP, 1979).

2. Stallings in McClintock and Lowenthal, eds., *The Peruvian Experiment Reconsidered*, p. 168.

3. Barbara Stallings, "International Influence on Economic Policy: Debt, Stabilization and Structural Reform," in Stephen Haggard and Robert Kaufman, eds., *The Politics of Economic Adjustment* (Princeton: Princeton University Press, 1992), pp. 41–88.

4. Stallings in Haggard and Kaufman, eds., *The Politics of Economic Adjusment*, pp. 48–58.

5. Carol Wise, "Peru Post-1968: The Political Limits to State-Led Economic Development," (Ph.D dissertation, Department of Political Science, Columbia University, 1990), p. 187.

6. Portocarrero, *Crisis y Recuperación*, p. 99.

7. This point is made by Peter Evans, "The State as Problem and Solution: Predation, Embedded Autonomy and Structural Change," in Haggard and Kaufman, eds., pp. 139–181.

8. A contract signed in 1981 between the government and the Superior Oil Company was criticized for its generous terms toward the multinational. When the army openly objected, President Belaúnde agreed to renegotiate its terms, no doubt recalling the army's unease over a previous oil contract that had contributed to his overthrow in 1968. This was the first and last time during the decade that the military vetoed an economic policy decision taken by the civilian regime. *Latin American Regional Reports: Andean Group*, August 1981, p. 2.

9. *Latin American Regional Reports*, October 1981, p. 1.

10. *Latin American Regional Reports*, December 1982, p. 2.

11. See especially *Caretas*, December 13, 1982, pp. 12–15.

12. Wise, "Peru Post–1968: The Political Limits to State-Led Economic Development," p. 189.

13. The most notable cases of alleged financial corruption included the "*caso Vollmer*" (1982) involving Prime Minister Manuel Ulloa and Justice Minister Felipe Osterling; the "*caso Guvarte*" (1983) involving Justice Minister Elias LaRosa; and the "*caso Bancoper*" (1983) involving Interior Minister José Rodríguez Pastor. Charges of nepotism were fostered by the key positions occupied by Belaúnde's family members. Belaúnde was linked by family with Ulloa and with ministers Ericson and García Belaúnde while Belaúnde's brother, Francisco, was president of the Chamber of Deputies.

14. Michael Reid, *Peru: Paths to Poverty* (London: Latin American Bureau, 1985), p. 83–4; Wise, "Peru Post-1968: The Political Limits to State-Led Development," p. 228.

15. Teresa Tovar, *Movimiento Popular y Paros Nacionales* (Lima: DESCO, 1982), p. 15.

16. APRA leader Haya de la Torre praised the military regime for offering "all the guarantees it can" for the elections. *Marka*, January 19, 1978, p. 16.

17. For a detailed analysis of the results, see Jorge Nieto, *Izquierda y Democracia en el Perú: 1975–1980* (Lima: DESCO, 1983); and Fernando Tuesta, "Análisis del Proceso Electoral a la Asamblea Constituyente," unpublished manuscript, (Lima: Universidad Católica, 1979).

18. See Nieto, *La Izquierda y Democracia en el Peru*, p. 89–99; Francisco Moncloa, "La Constitución, El APRA y el Nuevo Modelo de Dependencia," *Cuadernos Socialistas* 3, February 1980, pp. 12–24; and *Marka*, August 9, 1979, p. 24.

19. Unión Democrático Popular (UDP), "UDP: Balance y Tareas," (Lima: UDP, 1978), p. 8.

20. Jorge Parodi, *La Desmovilización del Sindicalismo Industrial Peruano Durante el Segundo Belaúndismo* (Lima: Instituto de Estudios Peruanos, 1986), p. 8.

21. Carmen Rosa Balbi, "Sindicalismo y Concertación," *Socialismo y Participación* 38, June 1987, p. 77.

22. See Chapters Seven and Eight.

23. Eduardo Figari, cited in Fernando Tuesta, *El Nuevo Rostro Electoral: Las Municipales del 83* (Lima: DESCO, 1985), p. 77.

24. See Chapter Six for a detailed discussion.

25. Centro Latinoamericano de Trabajo Social (CELATS), "Manual de Organización y Funciones de los Comedores Populares de El Agustino," (Lima: CELATS, 1983), p. 6.

26. Julio Andrés Rojas Julca, *Gobierno Municipal y Participacion Ciudadana: Experiencias de Lima Metropolitana, 1984–1986* (Lima: Friedrich Ebert, 1989), p. 32.

27. Serge Allou, *Lima en Letras* (Lima: CIDAP-IFEA, 1989), p. 74; Also see Nora Galler and Pilar Nuñez, *Mujer y Comedor Popular* (Lima: SEPADE, 1989); Luis Chirinos, "Gobierno Local y Participación Vecinal: El Caso de Lima Metropolitana," *Socialismo y Participación* 36, December 1987, pp. 1–27.

28. See Susan Stokes, "Politics and Latin America's Urban Poor: Reflections from a Lima Shantytown," *Latin American Research Review*, 26:2, pp. 75–102.

4

The Failures of State Populism

After nearly a decade of neoliberal economic policies, Peru in 1985 turned toward populism. Neoliberalism significantly weakened state capacities by accentuating social conflict, increasing bureaucratic inefficiencies, and reducing resources. A charismatic new president, Alan García, promised a reassertion of state power vis-à-vis the international lending agencies and banks that had exercised so much influence over economic policy making for a decade. As happened during the Velasco regime, the state under García was to reorder societal relations and redistribute economic wealth. But unlike the Velasco experiment in which state elites directed a "revolution from above," García's APRA party program called for the state to be a promoter of class compromise. State populism meant that the state was to reconcile interests, not to direct structural change. Even though García's populist project was different from Velasco's mobilization project, it suffered from some of the same limitations.

García's populism strongly resembled the populist politics practiced throughout most of Latin America during the first half of the twentieth century.[1] Such populist movements as those of Perón in Argentina, Velasco Ibarra in Ecuador, and Vargas in Brazil were based on a multi-class alliance between middle sectors, industrialists, and the urban working class. These were forged by the personal charisma of a central leader and guided by a vague ideology of reform and redistribution of wealth. The populist political project focuses on the state as an instrument of change. Through the state, economic reforms were carried out that favored investments meant to curtail the powers of foreign multinationals. The state also played a role in distributing benefits and favorable policies for allies. This may have meant, for example, keeping food prices in the cities low through subsidies or setting tariff barriers high to protect domestic industrialists. Populism also emphasized social control, especially of mobilized popular sectors, usually through strong authoritarian measures. The strong-arm tactics of the Peronist labor unions in Argentina or Vargas' labor code in Brazil typified this type of politics.

The populist model in Peru adopted under García fell victim to a state apparatus ill-equipped for the tasks of social control, reconciliation, and redistribution. This chapter will argue that state populism failed in Peru as a result of some of the same factors that undermined the Velasco mobilization project: the lack of cohesion among state elites, the inability of the state to influence or control newly mobilized sectors of society, and an unfavorable international environment that limited available resources to the state. Under Velasco and García, policy choices were out of sync with the limits of state power, and their implementation exacerbated the crisis of state power in Peru. After examining the nature of the populist coalition under García, this chapter will analyze how the interplay of the above factors helped bring a tragic end to yet another Peruvian experiment.

The Populist Coalition, 1984–1987

The shift of the APRA party back toward its populist roots after nearly three decades of conservative leadership was a slow and tortuous process that responded to the changed realities of Peru in the late 1970s and the death of Haya de la Torre, the party's leader and founder.[2] In the labor movement, a bastion of APRA organization since the 1930s, the APRA confederation (CTP) in 1980 represented less than 10 percent of organized labor. Without clear leadership and with its old popular sector base attracted to new leftist parties, APRA suffered a stunning political defeat in the 1980 presidential elections. APRA thus entered the 1980s as a mass party without control of any significant mass organizations and was hamstrung by its image of having been allied with traditional oligarchic parties.

After its 1980 defeat, the party was torn between its traditional leaders and a new renovating sector led by Secretary of Organization Alan García Pérez. García's rise in the party had been meteoric, helped by his fiery rhetoric and the close relationship he developed with Haya de la Torre during the latter's final years. The search in the party for a renewed discourse and image cleared the way for the charismatic and determined García.[3] At the party's 14th national congress in October 1982, García was elected APRA's secretary general after negotiating the support of traditional leaders. His new position confirmed him as the heir to Haya de la Torre and the APRA candidate for the next presidential election.

Beyond a youthful and charismatic image, García provided APRA with a new populist discourse based on the party's two traditional ideological pillars: the forging of a multi-class alliance and nationalism.[4] The slogan "a commitment to all Peruvians," that promised incentives to business and jobs for the poor, had a strong appeal in the crisis years of the early 1980s. García's populist discourse coopted the left's talk of change and help for the poor without antagonizing the middle sectors who felt threatened by the more radical elements of the United Left. APRA could, therefore, present itself as a unifying force among sectors threatened by Belaúnde's economic policy:

> Middle sectors and employees are becoming increasingly impoverished, and the global productivity of the country is declining in a 'bottleneck' of restricted consumption and demand for imports. At the same time, there is a growing injustice in the distribution of income, while there are increases in speculative enrichment, corruption, abuse. ... [5]

This same element of unity was present in García's nationalist rhetoric. He argued that the country's economic crisis was the result of IMF austerity measures and burdensome debt payments. By insisting on timely payments of debt obligations, García argued, international lenders were controlling the country's destiny and keeping the economy in recession. His nationalist economic message appealed to the poor as well as the business sector, which saw little benefit in continuing austerity if it merely prolonged the recession.

Over a full year before the elections, opinion polls gave García an ample margin of victory, versus the lowest approval rating yet for Belaúnde and his policies. García's strong personality appeared to dominate the campaign and his rivals seemed unable to break the aura of inevitable triumph that surrounded him.[6] A carefully designed media campaign projected a youthful, energetic "Alan," dedicated to national unity and renewal, through images that offered a sharp contrast to the elderly and detached Belaúnde. García's nearest rival was United Left's Alfonso Barrantes, who was ideologically close to García but lacked both the latter's youthful charisma and sophisticated media campaign. The election results were no surprise. García won with 53 percent of the vote to IU's 24 percent and AP's 7 percent (see Table 3.4). Peru had apparently veered sharply left on the political spectrum and a new stage of populist politics was to begin.

The populist coalition that propelled García to the presidency was an electoral one, forged in the latter years of the Belaúnde administration and driven by a combination of media charisma and vague appeals. During the first two years of the García administration, efforts were made to convert this electoral coalition into a governing one by using state policies to please a variety of groups. Although this strategy produced political deadlock and a renewed economic crisis in later years, it was successful in the short-term.

García's first measure announced a limit on debt service payments to 10 percent of annual export earnings. With a de facto moratorium already in place during Belaúnde's last year in office, the limit was a simple recognition of the reality that Peru could not fully meet its debt payments. But unlike Belaúnde, García attempted to use the debt issue to his own advantage, domestically and internationally. By taking the most radical stance in the region at the time (outside of Cuba's), García attempted to reassert the Peruvian state's leverage with the international financial system, and thus turn relative weakness into strength.[7] The administration calculated that the banks' fear of others following Peru's example, as well as the obvious inability to collect more than the amount set out by the state, would force the banks to accept a deal on Peru's terms. Domestically, García used the issue to rally nationalist sentiment, and to convince elites that monies used to pay international banks could be better invested to spur economic growth. It was an argument few at the time questioned. Nonetheless, it soon became evident that both international conditions and domestic factors would make the García approach economically costly for the country.

During his first year in office, García stimulated the economy by significantly increasing subsidies to business and labor and enacting a complicated system of price controls. All of the new "heterodox" policies, from price and exchange controls to increased social spending, emphasized selective state intervention in the economy. The stimulative effect of these policies appeared to work. In the next two years, the GNP grew a fantastic 8 percent per year, wages rose steadily, and inflation seemed to be under control.[8] Not surprisingly, García's popularity soared. His public approval rating reached over 90 percent by the end of his first six months, and the media remained fixed on his public doings, from his fondness of bellowing operatic arias to the weekly *balconazos* (speeches delivered from the palace balcony).

In practice, state interventionism under García amounted to dispensing "favors" to client members of the populist coalition. The state granted concessions and subsidies with the tacit condition of support for the regime. Thus, economic policy making was subordinate to the demands of coalition partners. The role of business sectors offers the clearest example of the clientelist uses of the state under García. Although the rhetoric of the new regime emphasized social redistribution and help for the poor, most of the state's direct assistance in Garcia's first two years went to the business sector. Such assistance included price subsidies, an artificially low dollar to support exports, tax credits for new investments, and multiple exchange rates to supposedly solve short-term import needs for machinery. Under this heterodox plan, business was expected to reinvest its profits from the resulting boom, thus sustaining the expansionary cycle started by state investment. To secure business support, García held informal meetings with the leaders of the twelve largest business groups, collectively known as the "twelve apostles."[9] Such leaders as Miguel Vega Llona, president of Peru's largest business association (CONFIEP), were often seen with García and boasted a close working relationship. Given García's populist rhetoric, the continuous consultations with business leaders over the administration's economic program appeared incongruous and both sides denied an "alliance" between business and the government existed. Nevertheless, it was clear that much of the success of García's economic program depended upon the cooperation of business.

The goal of the state populist model was to limit the social conflict and growing class polarization sparked by neoliberal policies. Key to the success of this populist experiment in Peru, as elsewhere, was the notion of a "benefactor" state that could satisfy the demands of all social sectors and demonstrate that a reconciliation of class interests was possible. The weakness of the model lay in the state's inability to simultaneously carry out such programs.

The first hint of difficulties came from the growing clamor in the labor sector against the regime. In May 1987, the police force went on strike, leaving the army to protect the streets of Lima. This coincided with the first general strike called by the CGTP under the García administration. It was officially called to protest stagnating wages but was also an attempt by radicals in the United Left to distance themselves from García. They feared that García had appropriated their radical rhetoric and that IU leader Alfonso Barrantes, a friend of García's, was not forceful enough in preserving the opposition identity of the coalition.

These strikes, however, demonstrated more than just the political calculations of party leaders. They also exposed the soft underbelly of the entire state populist project. Despite its overwhelming electoral victory in 1985 and again in the 1986 nationwide municipal elections, APRA still did not control any major mass organizations. Unions, peasant federations, and shantytown organizations remained in the hands of the United Left, a direct legacy of the Velasco era. Thus, García's populism lacked what most populist regimes, such as Perón's, based their power upon—control of important mass organizations. The consequences of this situation were apparent for APRA after its first two years in power. Without this control, APRA could not prevent or weaken the wave of social protests.

The lack of social control was accompanied by a state elite heavily politicized and increasingly corrupt. García came to office with a shadow cabinet in place and policy review commissions set up a full year before the 1985 elections. But along with a core group of technocrats, the new government included old style political cronies, trained in the clientelist practices that had allowed APRA to survive on the margins of power for over four decades. When the new Minister of Energy and Mines, Wilfredo Huayta, boasted that APRA would remain in power for fifty years, many suspected he meant APRA would use the state as a clientelist tool for the next fifty years. As a party excluded from control of the executive branch for so long, strong internal pressures and demands existed to use their new-found power for partisan political purposes, especially with policies that dealt with the poor. It was a small step from clientelism to open corruption and during the García period charges of corruption by state officials were widespread.

An additional element in the deteriorating situation of state elites was the growing internal APRA rivalries and the disruptions in policy making these caused. In June 1987, Prime Minister Luis Alva Castro resigned his position as secretary general of APRA. A rival of García, he was viewed by most as a likely heir. As García's former minister of finance, Alva was an architect of the regime's economic policies and his resignation came at a time when growth was slowing and inflation rising. For most observers, his resignation created a sense of instability and appeared to be politically timed.[10] García publicly opposed Alva's resignation and the dispute led to continued sparring that haunted the remainder of García's term.

A final factor limiting the possible success of the state populist project was the economic vulnerability of the Peruvian state. García's heterodox economic policies increased state spending in the hope that public monies would spur new investments and begin a cycle of economic recovery. Resources that would have otherwise been set aside for debt servicing were dedicated to public spending programs. García and his key economic advisors, such as Daniel Carbonetto, believed that together with subsidies, favorable exchange rates, and new protective tariffs, a public spending program would lay the basis for an economic take off. The Achilles heel, however, was the belief that public spending would lead to greater private investment. As major public projects, such as the metro system in Lima, were eating away at the country's reserves, the hoped for private investment failed to materialize.[11] This failure was aggravated by the earlier "10 percent solution" for the foreign debt. Rather than viewing the "10 percent solution" as part of a broad strategy to deal with the debt, the García administration saw it as solving the issue. The result was a complete cut off of dialogue with international creditors and of credit. As other nations in the region, including Mexico and Argentina, reached agreements with banks and lending agencies, Peru found itself isolated and its position with the banks significantly weakened.

Policy making during the García period focused on satisfying particular demands to maintain the loyalty of a specific group, even when serious economic costs were apparent. Concessions to the business sector to spur investments were often used for simple short-term speculative advantages. A typical example was the differential exchange rates set up to promote the importation of essential items. The so-called "MUC dollar" used to import these items was pegged often up to a third less than the official bank exchange rates. Within a short period of time, consumer goods and foodstuffs were imported using the MUC dollar and later sold on the streets of most cities at much higher black market exchange rates. The MUC dollar remained in place even when it became clear that it was being used for speculative ventures and not to further productivity or long-term investments.[12] More than economic and political pressures, the maintenance of the MUC dollar was primarily due to bureaucratic inertia and the parcelization of the state. Insofar as the benefits accrued to regime supporters in the business sector, policy makers were more than willing to look past the economic distortions the MUC dollar caused. Meanwhile, rumors and accusations circulated of regime officials involved in MUC dollar imports. The growing incoherence in policy making represented by the MUC dollar contributed to a sense of stagnation during 1987 and led to a re-evaluation of the economic program which questioned the entire coalition structure behind APRA's populism.

From Populism to Polarization, 1987–1989

Shifting Coalitions

The stagnation of APRA's populist project by mid-1987 set into motion a series of events and decisions that intensified the polarization of political society and effectively ended the populist experiment. Populism failed largely from an inability to transform the electoral coalition that propelled García to power into an effective governing coalition. Popular sector organizations distrusted the state and elite sectors saw the state primarily as a dispenser of subsidies and favors. In the absence of a multiclass alliance, populism under García relied almost solely upon his charisma.

As that charisma began to wear thin and the economy faltered, García searched for a way to shore up his declining image. In his July 1987 Independence Day speech, García announced the nationalization of banking, insurance, and financial institutions, excluding those directly foreign-owned. The decision essentially ended the state populist experiment. García struck out at what he saw as an irresponsible bourgeoisie, which benefitted from the administration's economic policies during the first two years but refused to reinvest its profits in productive domestic industries. While García calculated that his move would rally popular support, the nationalization split the ruling APRA, further radicalized the left, and reinvigorated a moribund right. The ensuing battle over the nationalization launched what became an ideological struggle over the shape of Peruvian society, with left and right questioning each others' legitimacy to participate in the democratic political game. As occurred during the Velasco regime, the state found it impossible to mobilize support in those sectors of society it thought were most amenable to its measures, given the preponderance and hostility of the left at the grassroots level. The state was also forced to confront the hostility of the upper-classes and the business sector. Armed with the anti-state liberal discourse that emerged in the post-Velasco era, these sectors mobilized vast resources against the prerogatives of the state.

The actual decision to nationalize the banks followed a pattern of decision making prevalent during the regime's previous two years. Bold decisions were made secretly among a small group of intimate advisors and revealed by surprise to the public and bureaucratic subordinates.[13] Only a handful of people knew in advance of the decision to nationalize the banks, and senior officials of APRA were not informed beforehand. Among Garcia's close advisors on this issue, such as Carlos Franco, none were linked to the party.[14] The public rationale for the decision was that the "financial oligarchy" had converted itself into a monopoly and had benefitted from economic growth but had not reinvested in the country, preferring to send profits abroad. García used very class-oriented language to describe the nationalization, arguing that it was a decision of the "people's government" against the rich who have "their pockets and stomachs full."[15]

García's bid to appeal to class loyalties proved fatal. It aroused the ire of the middle and upper-classes without achieving García's main goal: the support of the popular masses. Although García had been elected with lower-class support, voting support did not translate easily into mobilizable support for a policy issue. The inability to mobilize the support of popular sectors for this nationalization resulted from APRA's lack of significant lower-class organizations. García used mass rallies and the state broadcasting system to drum up support but the right's media campaign against the measure soon overwhelmed them. The left's ambivalent attitude also inhibited lower-class support. The United Left supported the "idea" of nationalization but opposed García's measure, echoing the right's worry of a "totalitarian" APRA that could abuse the power of the banks for partisan advantage.[16]

Nonetheless, the staunchest opposition to the measure arose from the right. The bank nationalization was seen as a direct threat to the participation of business and the middle-class in the country's political and economic system. The government's class-oriented rhetoric and its threats of further nationalizations if business did not meet national obligations raised fears of "another Velasco" dictatorship.[17] During the following years, García ominously alluded to the difficulties of carrying out structural changes in a democracy and of the power of the right to impede change. In one speech, after praising Velasco, García warned that revolution and democracy were incompatible and that his "revolutionary" program "cannot be applied under a democratic regime."[18]

Many of these fears became evident after the bank nationalization and especially during the right's 1990 presidential campaign. However, the first reactions to the nationalization focused upon the immediate political challenge. In mid-August 1987, at the urging of close friends including Hernando De Soto, director of Peru's leading right-wing think tank, the novelist Mario Vargas Llosa convoked an anti-nationalization rally. His call drew immediate support from all business groups as well as AP and the PPC. Far exceeding most expectations, these groups filled the massive Plaza San Martín, something the right had not done for several decades. That rally not only launched Vargas Llosa's political career but also inaugurated a new style of polarized politics. Vargas Llosa accused the government of lurching towards totalitarianism, threatening democratic continuity, and governing in alliance with the "communist" United Left. The crowd repeatedly shouted the pro-coup slogan *"Y va caer"* (He will fall) and carried signs denouncing "Apra-Communismo," a phrase widely used in the political persecutions of the 1940s.[19] For most observers, the rally was the Peruvian right's most ideologically charged discourse in decades.

From August 1987 through mid-1988, Peru's politics revolved around the nationalization issue. The media was saturated with anti-nationalization propaganda, and since all but the state television channel had links with the newly emerged right, news and political programming took on a decidedly anti-government tone. Both Vargas Llosa and García carried out public campaigns for their positions in what became a personal and ideological battle. Meanwhile, the actual nationalization was stalled due to challenges in the courts and the congress. Both sides used their individual influence and connections in the judicial system to get favorable rulings. A year after García announced the nationalization, the issue was virtually dead.[20] In the congress, the APRA majority divided over the issue. Sectors linked with the *"alvista"* wing of the party saw the issue as an opportunity to challenge García's undisputed leadership within APRA, thus preparing the way for Alva Castro to control the party before his 1990 presidential bid.

By early 1988 polarization was the predominant characteristic of Peru's political system. The center was weakening and the two ideological poles were moving to extreme positions.[21] The United Left moved further left as the moderate leadership was purged and the radical Partido Unificado Maríateguista (PUM) increased its influence. A newly invigorated right expanded its focus against what it called "Apra-Communismo," decrying the leftist legacy of the Velasco era and the influence of leftists in the political system.

Popular sector mobilization had created a large, impatient electorate which favored some form of structural change and redistribution. That was evident in the 1985 elections where both APRA and IU swept the political scene. The competition for this electorate that pitted APRA, IU, and their factions against each other created a tendency toward radicalism within these parties, as each tried to differentiate themselves by appearing more radical than their counterparts. Polarization from 1985 to 1987 was unidirectional toward the left. García's decision to nationalize the banks was part of this competition to maintain momentum and popular support. Hampered by his lack of organizational and easily mobilizable support among lower-class groups, García relied upon the typical instruments of populism, especially personal charisma and symbolism, to first win the presidency and then govern. The nationalization measure was a dramatic turn leftward in his administration when it became evident that his popular support was threatened by economic discontent, seemingly organized by the left. It was a fatal attempt to co-opt the left's support without seeing the possible consequences from the right.

Populist Austerity

From September 1988 through mid-1989, the García administration suffered a series of crises that created a high level of instability. When prominent banker Francisco Pardo Mesones suggested that García be "removed," most interpreted this as a call for a coup.[22] The threat of a military coup loomed larger than at any other time during the decade. Civilian politicians and journalists called for the president's resignation and García's own behavior raised questions about his personal stability.[23] The immediate spark to this new crisis was a series of economic adjustment policies announced in early September 1988, designed to reduce inflation and the fiscal deficit. Minister of Finance Abel Salinas drastically increased prices and cut subsidies in a way reminiscent of the IMF supported "*paquetazos*" that APRA had vehemently denounced during the Belaúnde administration. The result was an immediate recession, the outbreak of hyperinflation (see Table 4.1), and an acceleration of internal conflicts among regime policy makers. Together, these consequences virtually gutted a state apparatus already severely weakened by nearly a decade of neoliberal policies.

TABLE 4.1   Inflation and GNP Growth, 1985–1990

	1985	1986	1987	1988	1989	1990
Inflation (%)	158	63	114	1,722	2,775	7,650
GNP Growth (%)	1.7	10.8	9.7	–7.4	–12.3	–2.3[a]

[a] Estimated

Source: Inflation figures for 1985–89 from Carlos Paredes and Jeffrey Sachs, *Peru's Path to Recovery* (Washington D.C.: Brookings Institution, 1991), p. 85. 1990 inflation figure from *Sí*, January 6, 1992, p. 19; GNP figures from Ricardo Webb and Graciela Fernández–Baca, *Peru en Numeros* (Lima: Cúanto SA, 1991), p. 362.

One of the more vexing problems the need for an economic adjustment created was the conflict over policy implementation within the state bureaucracy. Policy making was divided among various groups who jealously guarded their access to power through García. While the ministry of economy was formally charged with economic policy making, most important policies emerged from a small group of informal heterodox advisors surrounding the president. Beyond these two contending groups was the central bank, with a tradition of independent policy making; the Instituto Nacional de Planificación (INP), that managed public investment projects; and the newly created Instituto de Comercio Exterior (ICE), charged with export and exchange rate policies. Although each agency guarded its policy making prerogatives, in this highly personalist regime where all power resided in the single charismatic figure at the top, major decisions were made by García himself. Those with the greatest access—the heterodox advisors—enjoyed the greatest influence. As the nationalization decision demonstrated, this system restricted debate and encouraged top-down decision making. In the face of a growing economic crisis, these divisions tended to produce inertia, as each group defended its own interests.

Inflationary pressures mounted as the government de-controlled many of the prices it had regulated during the high point of heterodoxy. Inflation for September 1988 reached 114 percent, with monthly rates averaging over 30 percent during the next year.[24] Hyperinflation, combined with the low confidence of business in the aftermath of the bank nationalization, helped push the country into the deepest recession in recent history. By 1989, 70 percent of the work force was either unemployed or underemployed, and those lucky enough to have maintained a job in the formal sector of the economy saw their wages and salaries severely reduced, amounting to only a third of their 1980 levels (see Table 4.2). Public sector employees were especially hard hit, with teachers seeing their monthly salaries drop to about US$30 a month. Such abysmally low salaries affected morale throughout all state bureaucracies, fostering corruption, absenteeism, and strikes. The most militant labor strikes of the late 1980s were among public sector workers, including the nearly six-month mine workers strike and strikes among municipal workers, teachers, and hospital workers.[25]

The decline in public employee wages was symptomatic of the overall collapse of state finances brought about by the economic crisis. Central government income in 1988 was nearly half its 1985 level as tax rates rapidly shrank. By 1990 taxes accounted for an historically low 4.9 percent of GNP, the lowest in Latin America.[26] The shrinking tax base reflected the effects of hyperinflation and the shift of income from the tax-paying formal sector to the tax-evading informal sector. In addition, the state's capacity to even collect taxes had diminished considerably (see Table 4.3). It was common knowledge among Lima businessmen that no one had ever been sent to prison for tax evasion and while the state had a right to shutdown businesses for tax evasion, no major businesses had ever been affected. The right "connection" was always seen as a way of avoiding such penalties. The García administration was also hit with a number of highly publicized corruption scandals. One of the most well-known cases involved Minister of Agriculture Remigio Morales Bermúdez (son of the ex-president), who was forced to resign in a scandal over kickbacks for importing rotted beef from Argentina. The atmosphere of alleged corruption was so pervasive it touched President García who was accused of kickbacks and the use of illegal funds to purchase real estate.[27] Beyond the accusations themselves, the growing perception of corruption at the highest levels significantly reduced state authority.

Along with the calls for the president's resignation came the threats posed by military interventions and persistent violence. A month after the announcement of the *"paquetazo,"* an attempted coup was aborted when a regional commander with conspicuous links to the García administration was removed by the joint command of the armed forces for plotting a coup.[28] The strongest coup rumors occurred in January 1989 when reports indicated that only a strong warning from the U.S. ambassador had dissuaded coup plotters.[29]

The tense atmosphere caused by these rumors and plots was accompanied by a sharp rise in the level and extent of political violence. The growing violence of Sendero Luminoso, paramilitary groups, and the military, raised serious questions about the state's ability to control violence. These problems also caused conflicts in the state apparatus, raised economic costs, and questioned the legitimacy of the state and its relation

TABLE 4.2   Changes in Real Wages and Employment, 1985–1989 (% change)

	1985	1986	1987	1988	1989
Real Wages					
Blue Collar	–17.2	37.0	10.0	–23.5	–45.0
White Collar	–11.2	29.2	5.5	–21.6	–47.6
Government Employees	–20.4	4.2	13.2	–2.2	–46.2
Minimum Wage	–12.6	3.7	8.7	–15.3	–51.7
Employment	–1.3	6.0	7.8	–1.5	–10.9

Source: Adapted from Carlos Paredes and Jeffrey Sachs, *Peru's Path to Recovery: A Plan for Economic Stabilization and Growth* (Washington D.C.: Brookings Institution, 1991), p. 85.

TABLE 4.3   Tax Revenue (as a percentage of GNP), 1979–1989

	1979	1981	1983	1985	1987	1989
Direct Taxes	6.7	4.8	2.9	2.4	2.1	1.3
Indirect Taxes	8.5	8.9	8.1	10.5	6.4	4.1
Other	0.7	0.6	0.5	1.0	0.2	0.6
Total	15.8	14.3	11.5	14.0	8.7	6.0

Source: Authors elaboration from Instituto Nacional de Estadisticas, as reported in *La República*, March 14, 1990, p. 12.

with society. The pressures were enormous on existing actors to adopt violent tactics. Many popular sector organizations faced strong competition on their left flank from Sendero. Through *"clasista"* front groups, Sendero promoted tactics such as indefinite strikes and factory takeovers as alternatives to those followed by IU-linked groups. The quandary many unions, peasant communities, and shantytown organizations faced was to either radicalize and adopt confrontational strategies or face the possibility of having their influence reduced.

Organized labor provides a good example of this dynamic. The initial reaction from unions to the decline in wages was an increase in strikes in 1987 and 1988. The CGTP called five national strikes during 1988, the highest number ever called in one year. Yet of the five, only two were clearly successful. Workers were apparently not willing to forego a day's salary during an economic crisis in order to register a symbolic protest.

Unions also faced competition from the labor organizations set up by Sendero to act as an alternative to the IU-controlled labor movement. Sendero's activity was concentrated along the Central Highway, Lima's industrial belt.[30] Union leaders linked to the CGTP were called "revisionists" and threatened. Local mine union leaders in Cerro de Pasco and Huancavelica were labeled traitors and assasinated by Sendero when they proposed ending strikes. Prolonged and violent strikes were a mechanism to instill consciousness and provide an opportunity for the party to organize among strikers.[31]

After 1987, IU-linked unions radicalized their actions, using more labor strikes that were longer and often violent. This was especially true for the large labor federations representing teachers, miners, and civil construction workers. Unlike smaller unions, the large federations were better organized and prepared to endure long strikes during the economic downturn. Each of these federations held strikes which lasted over sixty days during 1988 or 1989 and were characterized as some of the most violent in Peru's recent labor history. Strikers marching through the streets of downtown Lima routinely burned tires, hurled stones, and battled police. During the January 1990 civil construction strike, strikers barricaded themselves in their Lima headquarters and waged an open gunfight with the police that lasted several hours.[32] One of the longest and bloodiest strikes was the 1988 miners strike. The ninety-day strike

TABLE 4.4   Labor Strikes, 1980–1990

Year	Number of Strikes	Man Hours Lost (millions)
1980	739	17.9
1981	871	19.9
1982	809	22.7
1983	643	20.3
1984	516	13.9
1985	579	12.2
1986	648	16.9
1987	726	9.1
1988	815	37.9
1989	667	15.2
1990	613	15.0

Source: Figures from Webb & Fernández-Baca, *Perú en Numeros*, p. 324.

cost the country $5 million a day in lost export revenue and several mine leaders lost their lives as a result of actions by Sendero and security forces. Miners marched on Lima and battled police before several hundred were hurt or detained. Despite government promises that helped end the strike, union demands went largely unsatisfied and provoked additional actions the following year.

The growing sense of polarization and disintegration reached a high point during the 1990 presidential election campaign, the most polarized election in Peru since the 1930s. The class and racial cleavages which predominated in elections since 1978 were also evident, but accentuated by the political polarization of the García period. The result was a campaign that turned into a virtual referendum on national, social, and political identity. In the first round of the elections, the traditional parties put forward highly ideological proposals. Yet continuing a trend that emerged in the 1989 municipal elections, popular sectors rejected the traditional parties of the left in favor of "independent" candidates who promised stability and efficiency.[33] The second round of the elections pitted the unknown independent, Alberto Fujimori (Cambio 90), against the candidate of the rightist coalition FREDEMO, Mario Vargas Llosa.

The second round results demonstrated clear divisions along racial, class, and regional cleavages. FREDEMO lost all departments in the country except the Amazonian department of Loreto. From the APRA strongholds on the northern coast to the more leftist southern highlands, Fujimori won with margins that in some cases surpassed 70 percent of the vote. In Lima, Fujimori swept all lower-class districts with similar mar-

TABLE 4.5   Election Results, 1990 (percentage of total vote)

Party	First Round	Second Round
Fredemo	27.6	33.9
Cambio 90	24.6	56.5
APRA	19.2	
IU	7.0	
IS	4.1	
Others	2.2	
Blank	8.0	1.7
Null	7.3	7.8

Source: Jurado Nacional de Elecciones as reported in Fernando Rospigliosi, "Polarización Social y Desprestigio de los Partidos Políticos," unpublished manuscript (1991), p. 50.

gins. Vargas Llosa only carried Lima's middle and upper-class districts, where he won over 60 percent of the vote.[34] His rightist coalition's failure to broaden its appeal beyond the narrow urban middle-class vote proved fatal.

Conclusion

Five years after García's state populist experiment began, Peru appeared to be on the brink of a general collapse. Confronting its worst economic crisis, the country was isolated internationally because of its stand on the debt issue and besieged by growing political violence and polarization. An attempt to increase the state's resources and its influence in society ended in disarray. Like Velasco's corporatist revolution from above, Garcia's state populist experiment foundered on a series of problems that have repeatedly limited state capacity in Peru. By the late 1980s, the state was in a considerably weaker position in all key power arenas than it had been a decade earlier.

In the international arena, what initially appeared to be a bold reassertion of state prerogatives over international financial institutions ended by underscoring the economy's continued dependence on international markets. By 1987 Peru had been cut off from fresh funds due to its unilateral 10 percent solution and state revenue was rapidly shrinking. To the dismay of García's policy makers, no other Latin American country followed its lead on the debt, leaving Peru isolated as other nations moved toward debt renegotiations. Peru had little leverage to impose its policies on the banks. This stalemate need not have continued, however, if García had adopted a more flexible attitude and agreed to renegotiate Peru's position. Ultimately it was the specific policy choice to adopt the 10 percent solution and than remain with it, that was responsible for the state's weakened position.

Specific policy choices were also to blame for the deteriorating organizational resources of the state. Price, tax, and exchange rate policies, were very costly to the state, but were maintained primarily for a political reason—to preserve the populist coalition. Despite these policies, the coalition had come apart by the middle of García's term. The APRA party never quite won the loyalty of popular sectors and support from business elites was highly conditional and soon lost in the furor over the bank nationalization. Moreover, state efficacy was hindered by the extensive use of political cronyism, clientelism and corruption at all levels of the bureaucracy.

Probably the most ambitious aspect of the populist project was the effort to increase the state's influence in society by positing the state as the reconciler of interests. Ironically, by the end of the García period society was far more polarized than it had been in the mid-1980s. As most populist regimes find out quickly, it is extremely difficult to reconcile interests in a shrinking economy. The APRA regime found this especially difficult because its political influence among major social groups was minimal. It controlled few mass political organizations and, as the Velasco regime discovered, a distribution of resources in society without control of mass organizations is just as likely to benefit political opponents as supporters. Moreover, after 1987 there were few resources to distribute. Without incentives, populist practices proved ineffective in influencing societal organizations.

Notes

1. See Torcuato Di Tella, "Populism and Reform in Latin America," in Claudio Veliz, ed., *Obstacles to Change in Latin America* (London: Oxford University Press, 1965), pp. 47–74; and Michael Conniff, *Latin American Populism in Comparative Perspective* (Albuquerque: University of New Mexico Press, 1982). Much of the literature on populism has linked it to the problems of economic underdevelopment and the specific timing of industrialization. For an outline and critique of this argument see David Collier, ed., *The New Authoritarianism in Latin America* (Princeton: Princeton University Press, 1978).

2. The changes in APRA politics during the 1970s are examined in Mariano Valderrama, ed., *El APRA: Un Camino de Esperanzas y Frustraciones* (Lima: El Gallo Rojo, 1980). For shifts in party politics during the 1980s, see Carol Graham, *Peru's APRA* (Boulder: Lynne Reinner, 1992).

3. Many of the insights of this section were provided through conversations with Ricardo Ramos Tremolada, a former leader of APRA's youth sector during García's rise to power.

4. The basic texts of APRA's ideology are Victor Raúl Haya de la Torre, *El Anti-Imperialismo y el APRA* (Lima: APRA, 1986), and *Treinta Años de Aprismo* (Lima: APRA, 1986). A fascinating text where García offers his interpretation of Aprista ideology is in Alan García Pérez, *El Futuro Diferente: La Tarea Histórica del APRA* (Lima: EMI Editores, 1987).

5. García Pérez, *El Futuro Diferente*, p. 36.

6. Early poll results reported in *Caretas*, December 3, 1984, p. 12.

7. The best analysis of the issues surrounding García's decision is found in Drago Kisic, *De la Corresponsabilidad a la Moratoria: El Caso de la Deuda Peruana, 1970–1986* (Lima: Friedrich Ebert, 1987).

8. For an explanation and defense of heterodox policies in Peru see Daniel Carbonetto, *Un Modelo Económico Heterodoxo: El Caso Peruano* (Lima: Instituto Nacional de Planificación, 1987). A critique of these policies is found in Henry Pease García, "El Populismo Aprista: Ni Reformas, ni Revolución." *QueHacer* 47, July 1987, pp. 44–50. See also Ricardo Lago, "The Illusion of Pursuing Redistribution Through Macropolicy: Peru's Heterodox Experience, 1985–1990," in Rudiger

Dornbusch and Sebastian Edwards, eds., *The Macroeconomics of Populism in Latin America* (Chicago: University of Chicago Press, 1991), pp. 263–330.

9. The business "groups" are a set of diverse companies directed by one family. Among the largest groups are those run by the Romero, Brescia, Picasso, Wiese, and Pardo families. For a good discussion of business-government relations during the García regime see Francisco Durand, *Business and Politics in Peru* (Boulder: Westview Press, 1994).

10. *Sí*, July 13, 1987, pp. 6–9; Ricardo Ramos Tremolada, "El APRA en Vísperas de su XVI Congreso," *QueHacer* 53, July 1988, pp. 24–33.

11. Julio Gamero, "Cómo y Pórque se Gestó la Crisis: Del Shock Heterodox al Ajuste Ortodoxo," *QueHacer* 55, October 1988, p. 16; and Efraín Gonzales de Olarte, *Economia para la Democracia* (Lima: Instituto de Estudios Peruanos, 1989).

12. See Oscar Dancourt, "Sobre la Hyperinflación Peruana," *Economia* 12, 1989, pp. 13–44.

13. Among those decisions were the moratorium on debt payments, the reorganization of the police force, and the creation of the defense ministry. This interpretation is sustained by the semi-autobiographical account of García found in Guillermo Thorndike, *La Revolución Imposible* (Lima: EMI Editores, 1988).

14. In an interview several weeks before the nationalization, Franco told this author that García's first two years had not been truly "revolutionary" and that the administration needed to take "bold" actions to prove its radical credentials. Interview by author in Lima, July 14, 1987. Franco, along with Daniel Carbonetto, had been a member of the SINAMOS planning board.

15. *La República*, August 17, 1987, p. 3; and *Caretas*, August 10, 1987, pp. 12–18.

16. *La República*, August 15, 1987, p. 5.

17. These fears were aggravated by García's warning that further nationalizations were likely. *La República*, August 11, 1987, p. 4.

18. *La República*, July 2, 1989, p. 2.

19. Author's eyewitness account, August 26, 1987.

20. *Actualidad Económico*, April 1988, p. 14.

21. For a theoretical discussion of polarization see Giovanni Sartori, *Parties and Party Systems* (Cambridge: Cambridge University Press, 1976), pp. 135–136.

22. For a good summary of instability in this period see Marcial Rubio, "Las Danza de Ilusiones," *Debate* 53, 1988, p. 8–10.

23. Among the politicians calling for García's resignation were PPC leader Luis Bedoya Reyes, PUM leader Javier Diez Canseco, and prominent journalists such as César Hildebrandt. García's stability was questioned when at the height of the political crisis he disappeared from public view for a month. See *Sí*, September 28, 1988, p. 4.

24. Manuel Pastor and Carol Wise, "Peruvian Economic Policy in the 1980s," *Latin American Research Review* 27:2, 1992, p. 106.

25. Carmen Rosa Balbi, "Estrategias Obreras: La Recesión Silenciosa," *QueHacer* 59, 1989, pp. 12–22.

26. *La República*, October 9. 1990, p. 10.

27. In 1991 the parliamentary immunity that the former president enoyed was lifted by congress as a result of persistent accusations of corruption. When the

Fujimori government attempted to arrest García in 1992, he fled to Colombia where he was granted refuge as a political exile.

28. *Sí*, October 17, 1988, p. 14; and *El Comercio*, October 15, 1988, p. 2. The close relation that General Victor Raúl Silva Tuesta enjoyed with the government and with APRA led to speculation that the planned coup was actually an attempted *autogolpe* by García to acquire dictatorial powers.

29. *La República*, February 21, 1989, p. 3.

30. *La República*, March 29, 1990, p. 37.

31. For Sendero's attacks on mines and the mine workers union see *La República*, July 23, 1989, p. 10. Insights into Sendero's actions towards the unions can be found in its newspaper. See *El Diario*, May 1988, p. 4.

32. On the wave of strikes see *La República*, November 11, 1988, p. 12. The strikes also resulted in violence against the unions from security forces and paramilitary groups. See *La República*, May 19, 1989, p. 8.

33. An explanation for the emergence of independents that stresses the role of an emerging "informal" economic sector is found in Maxwell Cameron, *Democracy and Authoritarianism in Peru* (New York: St. Martin's Press, 1994).

34. Official results as reported in *QueHacer* 65, August 1990, pp. 22–23.

5

Retooling the State:
The Fujimori Coalition
and State Reform[1]

Few observers expected Alberto Fujimori, an unknown ex-university rector, to eclipse the traditional political parties or the well-financed campaign of the internationally famed novelist Mario Vargas Llosa in the 1990 presidential elections. In fact, Fujimori capitalized effectively on broad disenchantment with established parties and the dramatic ethnic and economic divide separating Vargas Llosa's supporters from the rest of the country. Yet little was known of Fujimori's ideology, and his few speeches sounded a populist tone similar to those of García.[2] Shortly after taking office it became clear that his program would have a distinct neoliberal orientation. This chapter examines the coalition of interests—including the military, civilian technocrats, international financial agencies, and domestic business groups—that coalesced around Fujimori after his election and helped forge a neoliberal economic program meant to "rationalize" the state administrative apparatus and strengthen the authority and effectiveness of the military and other state agencies. Short-term stabilization was only the first step toward a broader reshaping of the economic rules of the game. All of these groups shared an interest in stabilizing the economy and getting it back into the international financial system, and they were averse to the populist and class-based politics that had predominated during the Velasco and García administrations. Strong consensus also existed on the need to adopt hard-line tactics to deal with Sendero Luminoso. Thus underlying the consensus on neoliberal policies and increased militarization was the recognition that both required a strengthened state apparatus.

Having been elected without an organized political party or any clear plan for governance, Fujimori quickly turned to a small group of civilian technocrats to fill key positions in the state bureaucratic structure. Hernando de Soto, director of the Instituto Libertad y Democracia (Peru's free-market think tank), was charged to use his international connections to renegotiate the foreign debt and later to redesign the strategy against narcotics.[3] Fujimori's turn towards technocratic elites to serve in the new administration also included appointing career bureaucrats known for their integrity to lead the inefficient and corrupt tax-collection agency SUNAT (Superintendencia Nacional de Administración Tributaria), the social security bureau IPSS (Instituto Peruano de Seguridad Social), and the customs agency SUNAD (Superintendencia Nacional de Aduanas). Other advisors were named to oversee plans to sell a number of state companies under the auspices of COPRI, the new Comisión de Privatización. The impetus for reconstructing the state bureaucratic structure after years of clientelist practice and inefficiencies was obvious. Moreover, some of these efforts yielded surprisingly good results in a relatively short time. As will be shown, all these agencies made significant advances in increasing their capabilities and resources.

By the end of Fujimori's first year in office, it became clear that civilian technocrats were only part of a much larger coalition of political actors interested in reconstructing the state apparatus. For example, international financial agencies wanted to see Peru "reinserted" into the international financial system, where it had been a pariah since the mid-1980s. By 1990, debt renegotiations for Latin America's largest debtors (including Mexico and Argentina) appeared to have diffused most talk of a confrontational strategy in the region. On the Peruvian side, this trend was reflected in the Fujimori administration's eagerness to carry out its reinsertion strategy. De Soto and Minister of Finance Carlos Boloña were anxious to reestablish Peru's credit and gain access to new funds, which were critical to the state rebuilding in infrastructure because significant investments had not been made since the early 1980s. The announcement by the Inter-American Development Bank in late 1991 of a credit of $220 million (the largest in nearly a decade) for highway construction and repairs was thus viewed as a major triumph for the reinsertion effort.[4]

Clearly, civilian technocrats and international lenders shared the goal of reordering the state along neoliberal economic lines. The IMF, the World Bank, and international banks were all encouraging the liberal agenda of privatization and orthodox policies throughout Latin America and were eager to see them implemented in Peru as well. With the perceived failures of populism and socialism, neoliberal economic thinking gained significant ground in the late 1980s throughout the region and clearly benefitted from the belief in a lack of viable policy alternatives.

Much the same logic appeared to be at work in Peru at the start of the Fujimori regime. Fujimori campaigned against the neoliberal policies espoused by Vargas Llosa, but once in office, he found his alternatives limited by the demands imposed by international agencies for renewing funds and the advice of liberal-minded technocrats like De Soto. Fujimori's policies on international reentry and neoliberal economics were especially appealing to the regime's third coalition partner, the business sector. The defeat of Vargas Llosa, whom it had backed assiduously, clearly disoriented the business sector. Fujimori's adoption of much of Vargas Llosa's neoliberal agenda, along with naming a pro-business prime minister soon after taking office, came as a pleasant surprise to business.[5] These developments were followed by close contacts and an effusive reception at the annual business congress, where Fujimori had been invited as the keynote speaker.

The cornerstone of Fujimori's state reconstruction coalition, however, was the Peruvian military. The military, as we shall see in a later chapter, had been directly affected by the state crisis of the 1980s. It entered the 1990s on the defensive against insurgency, highly demoralized, and stretched in its economic resources. Among the select corps of technocratic advisors that surrounded the new president were a small group of military advisors determined to establish its power base in the armed forces. Soon after the election, Fujimori isolated himself on a military base, reportedly planning his administration. Vladimiro Montesinos, a close advisor with special influence in the new administration, acted as a liaison between Fujimori and the armed forces and attended all meetings involving defense issues, even though he occupied no formal position.[6] Within weeks of taking office, Fujimori purged the police command and the interior ministry of those appointed by the García administration. Over the next year, he adroitly retired hostile military commanders (such as the commander general of the navy) and promoted a host of favorable officials, in an obvious effort to have an array of sympathetic officers in key positions.

Accompanying these personnel changes was a growing militarization of the effort to maintain public order and reassert state authority by using military troops for tasks that were normally left to the police. Throughout 1991, heavily armed troops were used to wipe away Sendero graffiti in the universities, to accompany the SUNAT in closing down street vendors who failed to pay taxes, to guard prisons, and to distribute food commodities in shantytowns. By mid-1991 many Peruvians were questioning the goals and plans of the new military powers. The military purges fueled rumors of a planned coup, which were vehemently denied by the administration.[7] Yet, the possibility of an authoritarian option loomed larger than at any point in the previous ten years.

The rapidity with which these interests coalesced around Fujimori, and the lack of an alternative political project largely reflected the collapse of the party system that had allowed Fujimori to win the presidency and then dominate the political agenda. That collapse, in turn, resulted in many ways from the same forces that had weakened the state in the 1980s. Although the popular class mobilization that took place in the 1970s brought the demands of a previously excluded sector into the political system via new forms of participation, these changes in civil society were not easily translated into changes in political society. The newly strengthened electoral left that emerged after the 1978 constituent assembly elections, did not benefit any single party that could consistently maintain the loyalty of this new sector. Hence the new popular classes just as easily supported APRA's Alan García in 1985, the independent Fujimori in 1990 and the leftist coalition, United Left (IU) in the 1983 municipal elections.[8] The difficulty in finding a representative outlet in political society for this new sector, reflected in part the fact the origins of political elites across the spectrum in the white, urban, upper middle classes. Organizational efforts at the grassroots, extensive in the IU, were hampered by the closed, cell-like structure of many parties that kept the party *"cúpulas"* (leadership) isolated from the mass bases.[9]

Beyond these structural problems lay the question of political efficacy. After a decade of electoral democracy, most of the country's political elite had participated in some form of governance, and thus in what was by then perceived as the failed policies of both the left and right during the 1980s. The lack of new faces among the leadership of the various parties reinforced this sense of exhaustion of political society.[10] Following their electoral defeat in 1990, the traditional parties failed to regroup or change their leaders or programs. Rather, during most of Fujimori's first year and a half in office, party leaders squandered their energies on internal disputes. The IU—ideologically bereft after the collapse of communism, besieged by Sendero, and racked by personalist conflicts—did little more than try to deflect blame for its disastrous performance in 1990. APRA and former President Alan García had been discredited in the eyes of most Peruvians by their catastrophic administration, and García remained under investigation for various financial scandals during most of this period. Fujimori skillfully played on APRA's weakness by initially trading favorable APRA votes in congress for placing limits on the investigation into García. On the right, the remnants of Vargas Llosa's FREDEMO, after watching Fujimori steal their neoliberal agenda, supported much of the administrations legislation while attempting to keep their political distance from a president who remained a social outsider to the close-knit network of right-wing parties.[11] Fujimori's own "party," Cambio '90, was hardly more than a personal electoral vehicle that had little influence in the executive, and won no significant governmental posts for its members.

Fujimori thus began his administration in the unique position of lacking a proper electoral party but having no single opposition figure or party confronting him.[12] The new president also benefitted from the fact that his potential opponents had seriously underestimated his political skills. Almost immediately, he began to confound observers and baffle public opinion by reaching out to the left, right, and center for political appointees, offering enticements that kept established players off guard. Thus, while implementing drastic economic "shock policies" and opening negotiations with international creditors, Fujimori also appointed well-known leftist leaders to cabinet posts and other high positions. In doing so, he kept many guessing about his "real intentions." But when it became clear that major policy decisions were made by Fujimori's closed circle of economic and military technocrats, with little outside influence, these appointees resigned.[13]

Neoliberalism and the New Authoritarian State

The Fujimori administration's attempt to strengthen the state apparatus was concentrated in two of the arenas of state power discussed earlier: state influence in society and the state's own organizational resources. In acknowledging the need for financial agreement with international lenders, the Fujimori regime revealed that its first priority was to enhance state power domestically and that mending its relations with international finance was a necessary condition for doing so. Enhanced capacities in both arenas, therefore, became key to the overall success of the Fujimori neoliberal reform program. Much higher levels of stability were required to spur investment and private sector activity, a goal that demanded eliminating the insurgent threat and dampening popular sector protests and challenges like those of the 1980s. Fujimori's response in this area was to emphasize the necessity for public order by strengthening the powers and resources of the security forces. Yet at the same time, in order to carry out this function and play a less direct role in economic management, the state must reorder its organization and resources significantly. The Fujimori administration clearly attempted to shift the state out of some economic activities while increasing its resources and enhancing its prerogatives in others. This is an important difference with the neoliberal reform undertaken during the Belaúnde administration. The Fujimori reformers did not confuse a reduced state role in the economy with a weak state, and recognized the need for strengthened state capacities in order to carry out broader reforms.

What is noteworthy with regard to this effort at neoliberal reform, in contrast to the rest of the region in the 1990's, is the authoritarian methods adopted to carry it out. This approach was evident even before Fujimori discarded democratic procedures completely. In late 1991, for instance, Fujimori used his legislative decree powers to enact 120 new laws, most pertaining to economic reforms, but a significant number granting new powers to the military. Together, these legislative decrees represented the most significant reordering of the Peruvian state since the Velasco era and demonstrated that the Fujimori administration was inter- ested in more than short-term stabilization. The decrees were aimed at eliminating the interventionist role of the state adopted during the Velasco years and enshrined in the Constitution of 1979. Most of the stric- tures in the 1969 agrarian reform on land sales, investments and manage- ment were reversed, along with laws regarding worker participation, union organization, job security, and sales of state property. Meanwhile, neoliberal economic reforms were accompanied by a series of authoritar- ian political decrees. Arguing that the military required expanded powers over civil society to combat insurgency, Fujimori proposed to grant the armed forces authority to tighten restrictions on journalists, confiscate property on the grounds of national security, create special military courts to try terrorist suspects, and ensure that no military officials could be tried in civilian courts for violating human rights.[14] Taken as a whole, the decrees thus embodied the two priorities of the new neoliberal authori- tarian state.

Bringing the Military Back In

The decrees dealing with national security antagonized many Peruvi- ans across the political spectrum, who accused Fujimori of attempting to restrict basic democratic freedoms. By early February 1992, the Peruvian Congress had overturned most of these decrees. The decrees themselves, however, were only the most publicized aspect of the broader effort to increase state control over society by giving security forces greater authority and new resources. At least two other measures underscored the new emphasis on state coercion.

First, the Fujimori administration revamped and amplified the role of the intelligence services. Every branch of the armed forces, along with the police, had its own intelligence agency, and they often worked at cross- purposes. Fujimori and advisor Vladimiro Montesinos relied heavily upon a reorganized National Intelligence Service (SIN) as the primary intelligence organ. Although information on budget and personnel changes are unavailable, strong indications have surfaced of Fujimori's propensity for using the SIN far more extensively to control political and civil society than any of his predecessors. A vast telephone espionage network aimed at opposition party members was created, along with efforts to influence media reporting of events, such as surreptitiously providing television reporters with supposed documentation of the November 1992 anti-Fujimori conspiracy among retired army officers.[15] Fujimori's willingness to use the SIN to alter public perceptions and keep track of opponents, broke sharply with the largely military role assigned to intelligence during the 1980s.

A second aspect of the effort to expand state influence in society via security forces was an ongoing militarization of counterinsurgency strategy. This trend led to an expanded role for the military in policing activities and organizing social groups to engage in counterinsurgency activity. As we shall see in Chapter Eight, both approaches were used during the Belaúnde and García periods, but Fujimori made them the centerpiece of his effort to stop the expansion of Sendero Luminoso. In addition to ceding greater authority to the military, Fujimori's counterinsurgency policy meant giving the armed forces a more visible role in maintaining public order. As was mentioned earlier, Fujimori used the military to occupy a number of universities, distribute food, conduct house-to-house searches for suspected *Senderistas* in shantytowns, and accompany SUNAT agents on their tax-collecting rounds. The greatest level of involvement, however, occurred when the military organized and armed "*las rondas*," self-defense committees established in the countryside and in the shantytowns. While they have a long previous history in Peru, it is only under the Fujimori administration that they came to occupy a central role in counterinsurgency and were encouraged on a wide scale.[16]

Small State, Effective State?

Most of the decrees issued by Fujimori in 1991 dealt with the economy and were aimed at transforming the nature of state intervention. The immediate outcome of these decrees was a reduction of state regulation and the size of the public sector as well as a weakening of popular-sector economic actors such as unions and producers, who formerly depended on state patronage. Before and after the April 1992 coup, Fujimori's neoliberal project of state reconstruction attempted to change the nature of the state's economic role by emphasizing privatization, restrictions on union activity, and a greater ability to collect taxes.

From the start of the Fujimori administration, it was clear that a significant effort would be made to privatize major parts of the public sector. In addition to privatizing some small state-owned banks, the administration concentrated its attention on the agricultural sector, disbanding cooperatives and allowing large- scale capital to enter the agrarian sector for the first time since the Velasco reform.[17] By 1992, attention was focused on the productive enterprises owned by the state. Over the next three years, the regime had sold off mining enterprises, the national airline, and the telephone company to private foreign investors. A final and more radical component of state divestiture has been the privatization of the social security system, using the Chilean model established during the regime of General Augusto Pinochet. Under the reforms, workers have the option of selecting retirement plans from private insurance companies, with little state regulation of these funds.[18]

The change in social security indicated a much broader shift in worker-state relations initiated by the Fujimori regime. Reversing the rights and benefits of organized labor acquired during the Velasco regime, and largely maintained even during the conservative Morales Bermúdez and Belaúnde administrations, the Fujimori regime curtailed the ability of unions to organize and protest.[19] In attempting to weaken union organizing, new decrees were enacted prohibiting unions from engaging in "political" activities. Additionally, workers could not organize more than one union in their workplace. Although regime supporters argued that this proviso would foster democratization in the union movement, the obvious purpose was to undermine the possibility of a unified labor movement. Other measures enacted included limits on the right to strike for public sector unions, the elimination of worker cooperatives and ending the mediating role of the ministry of labor in collective bargaining.

Labor's ability to contest these drastic changes imposed by the state was severely limited. First, the prolonged economic crisis crippled labor's ability to mobilize workers. By 1989, real wages were half of their levels in 1980, which were in turn half their level of the mid-1970s. Declining industrial production had forced many workers into the informal economy, which by 1990 accounted for more than two-thirds of the economically active population. As is often noted, the informal economy is very difficult to organize. These trends impaired the ability of unions to expand their membership and to urge workers (who correctly fear losing their positions or wages amid recession) to engage in effective collective action.[20] Another factor limiting worker responses has been their susceptibility to violence. After 1989, Sendero Luminoso carried out an extensive campaign to capture the union movement, infiltrating meetings and strikes and assassinating leaders who resisted their efforts. In response, security forces increasingly turned to repressing labor. The cost to labor in the early 1990s was very high, as was dramatized by the assassinations of mine union leader Saúl Cantoral and Pedro Huilca, the leader of the CGTP.

Although the Fujimori neoliberal reform project attempts to reduce the direct role of the state in productive functions through privatization, the administration's approach to labor demonstrates that this goal did not imply a weaker state role in the economy. In the area of taxation, the state significantly enhanced its capacities and expanded its ability to gather resources. One of the most effective of the new technocrats appointed by Fujimori was Manuel Estela, director of the tax collection agency SUNAT, from 1990 to 1992. Estela employed new powers ceded by Fujimori to crack down on tax evaders, including closing well-known businesses, increasing tax rates on individuals and property, and making highly publicized raids against street vendors who failed to comply with tax laws. The SUNAT's aggressive new policy achieved notable results, ending the precipitous decline in tax revenues that occurred in the 1980s. In 1991 tax revenue increased to more than 8 percent of the gross national product, climbing from its all-time low of just under 5 percent in 1989.[21]

Up to early 1992, Fujimori had adroitly managed the political scenario, keeping his opponents off guard, playing on the internal divisions and rivalries of the major political parties, and denouncing politicians, parties, the congress and the judiciary as corrupt and inefficient. For most Peruvians, these assertions contained enough truth to make Fujimori's attacks highly popular.[22] The rejection of many of Fujimori's decrees by the congress, however, signaled the first major setback in his neoliberal authoritarian project. It also represented the first clear assertion of opposition prerogatives in response to Fujimori's constant and popular attacks on the parties and congress as obstacles to reform.

The concern over a loss of initiative by Fujimori in early 1992 was underscored in the inaugural speech of the new president of the Comando Conjunto, General Nicolás de Bari Hermoza. Breaking with the strong "apolitical institutional tradition" of the armed forces predominant since 1980, the general stated that the military as an institution endorsed "each and every one" of Fujimori's decrees.[23] Open endorsement of a civilian president by a high- ranking military official was not only unprecedented, but a violation of the 1979 constitutional prohibition on military officials making "deliberative" comments. Yet this dramatic statement elicited only a mild reaction from most sectors, with no more than a few congressmen suggesting that he should be summoned to "explain" his comments. With an open ally heading the armed forces, the Fujimori administration clearly felt its base of support was as solid as ever. It was against this backdrop of firm support from the armed forces and growing doubts about the ability to sustain the state reconstruction project that Fujimori launched his *autogolpe*, or self-coup. In the early morning hours of April 5, 1992, tanks surrounded the Peruvian Congress, while troops detained leading opposition figures, journalists and judges. President Fujimori announced that constitutional democracy would be "temporarily" suspended until new rules and institutions could be created. The political order created in the aftermath of the 1978–1980 transition to civilian rule had come to an end.

Democracy and Neoliberal State Reform

Breaking Peru's fragile democratic rules, Fujimori decided to impose his state reconstruction project directly via authoritarian means, thus avoiding the possible obstacles and inevitable compromises democratic procedures imply. As has been shown, much of his administration's conduct indicated a disdain for democratic procedures and for political society in general. Yet to what extent was the turn to authoritarianism a necessary or inherent part of the neoliberal reconstruction policies? Many "liberals" in Peru and beyond pointed to the case of Chile under Pinochet to suggest that deep structural reforms along neoliberal economic lines require a period of authoritarian rule to be implemented effectively, given the entrenched resistance of established interests. Yet such reforms were being carried out elsewhere in Latin America and in Eastern Europe largely without negating fundamental democratic procedures.[24] In fact, the *autogolpe* caused serious new tensions and uncertainties within Fujimori's neoliberal reformist coalition.

The suspension of the constitution put critical strains on the very sectors that had coalesced around the president to rebuild the state. First came the withdrawal of international financial actors who had been such a crucial part of the regime's effort at restructuring the economy and the state. The United States led a group of international creditors in suspending all assistance to Peru, effectively halting the country's planned reentry and renewed access to foreign credit, a cornerstone of the government's program. Although international sanctions as severe as those imposed on Haiti after the overthrow of President Aristide were avoided, it was clear that the coup had precipitated international isolation. Peru's participation in such critical regional associations like the Rio Group and the Andean Pact were suspended, and several countries curtailed diplomatic ties, including Venezuela, Spain and Panama.

The hostile international reaction to events in Peru was not anticipated by regime officials. Fujimori argued that once international critics "understood" the reasons for the move, they would cooperate with the new authoritarian regime. What he failed to understand was that international actors responded by taking a hard-line against the suspension of democracy in Peru, because to have reacted otherwise could have encouraged similar authoritarian movements elsewhere in Latin America and in Eastern Europe.[25] As on previous occasions, decision makers in Peru undertook actions which were out of sync with global trends and pitted them openly against international actors. Given the Peruvian state's vulnerability in the international arena, in this case its need for new investments to complete the restructuring effort, the *autogolpe* appeared self-destructive. It caused a key member of the neoliberal coalition to end its support for the regime, at least temporarily. Moreover, efforts to reopen channels severed by the April coup were slow in coming, and were linked by the international community to holding new elections. The result was a significant delay in Peru's program to reenter the world market.

Fujimori's domestic partners supported the coup in its immediate aftermath, undoubtedly buoyed by opinion polls that demonstrated significant support for the move among major sectors of society. Yet even here, unity was more apparent than real. Hernando de Soto, who had played an important role in establishing new channels of communication between the regime and the international community had already left the administration several months earlier. While most business associations outwardly supported the *autogolpe*, a growing fear soon set in about the implications of the international aid cut off.

The institution most compromised by the neoliberal authoritarian move was the military. Its support effectively cemented a new politicization of the Peruvian armed forces as an institution. The civilian regime of Fujimori had manipulated and politicized the command structure of the armed forces to a degree unprecedented in recent Peruvian history and stood as a stark reminder of the deprofessionalization of the military during the 1980s. By aligning itself so closely with the new authoritarian regime, the military also provoked new divisions and factional disputes, as occurred during the Velasco era. A conspiracy in November 1992 among retired officers to depose Fujimori and restore the Constitution of 1979 was quickly followed by additional conspiracies among active-duty officers and a series of purges within the Army. Among those purged in early 1993 was General Rodolfo Robles, who had publicly linked the activities of paramilitary groups with the SIN and Vladimiro Montesinos.[26]

The somewhat shaky ground that the neoliberal economic coalition found itself standing on after the *autogolpe* reveals the most basic problem confronting any new authoritarian regime: its ability to institutionalize the changes it is seeking in the relationship among the state, society and the broader political system. All such regimes face the impossible problem of legitimating themselves in the eyes of a "world market place" where democracy predominates, and in a domestic environment where

authoritarian rule is perceived as transitory.[27] For the new authoritarian regime in Peru, this problem was especially difficult, given a hemispheric environment in which a democratic discourse now prevailed. Repeated missions sent by the Organization of American States underscored the need for a democratic solution, while the looming threat of further isolation and possible sanctions ultimately forced the regime to call for constituent assembly elections, which were held in November 1992. International pressure thus played a key role in forcing the Fujimori administration to abandon efforts to openly consolidate authoritarian structures of governance.

The capture of Abimael Gúzman, Sendero's founder and leader, in September 1992 bolstered Fujimori's popularity levels and led many to suggest that the regime could now acquire the capacity to legitimate its broader actions. While the importance of this capture cannot be underestimated in terms of legitimation of the regime and Peru's future welfare, the regime's ultimate ability to reshape the state-society dynamic remained to be seen. One need look no further than Peru during the Velasco regime to recognize the limits on authoritarian social transformation led by the state. The corporatist organizations created by the Velasco regime were designed "from above" and as a result largely failed to gain the allegiance of the social groups for whom they were created. Society essentially overwhelmed the structures built and imposed by the state and did so on the state's own terrain. Parties and new social organizations used the resources of the state for their own purposes, and by the late 1970s not a single pro-regime corporatist mechanism remained. The Fujimori policies and the coup they led to, a desperate response to the massive state crisis handed down from the 1970s have repeated the errors of past authoritarian attempts to reconstruct a state whose problems have deep roots in a history of injustice and inequality.

Confronted with the international isolation provoked by the *autogolpe* and the coalition's recognition that it did not automatically solve the country's most immediate problems, Fujimori found the possibilities of developing formal authoritarian structures limited. Nonetheless, his regime made important strides in creating new institutional arrangements that incorporated its neoliberal reforms and authoritarian methods via electoral means. The constitution adopted by the Constituent Assembly in mid-1993 and ratified by plebiscite discarded the "social market" orientation of the Constitution of 1979 in favor of an openly free-market agenda. The Constitution of 1993 also strengthens the powers of the executive: it created a unicameral legislature that can be dismissed by the president, increased control of the executive over the judiciary, provided for presidential reelection, and incorporated all of Fujimori's decrees rejected by the previous congress. By means of these new rules of the game, the regime hoped to create institutions that could guarantee the continuation of the neoliberal authoritarian experiment.

The reelection of Alberto Fujimori in the presidential elections of April 1995, promised yet another guarantee of that continuation. Fujimori handily defeated his main challenger, former United Nations Secretary General Javier Pérez de Cuellar, in the first round of voting with over 60 percent of the valid votes and also maintained his majority in congress.[28] The transition from the developmentalist state to the neoliberal authoritarian state seemed complete.

Conclusion

Fujimori's *autogolpe* of April 1992 was the culminating response of an attempt to restructure the state and its relations with society through a combination of neoliberal economic reforms and authoritarian political methods. These efforts have been supported by a coalition of interests— including technocratic elites, the military, business and the international financial community—that coalesced around Fujimori to reverse the structural decline in state capabilities taking place in Peru since the mid-1970s. Although each of these groups had its own agenda, the underlying logic of this coalition and the administration it supported was the necessity of strengthening the state in the areas required to carry out a neoliberal modernization of the economy and society. In the aftermath of the *autogolpe*, significant problems and tensions emerged, forcing the regime to abandon the openly authoritarian aspects of the project, while forging ahead in attempts to institutionalize the most significant structural changes adopted since 1990.

The different civilian regimes that governed Peru in the 1980s failed to resolve the entrenched structural problems facing the state and society. The state's inability to devise a sustainable development strategy that could provide growth and meet the basic needs of the population as well as its inability to reverse the declining capabilities of a state structure increasingly unable to maintain public order or assert its authority created enormous frustrations among all sectors of society. These frustrations paved the way for the emergence of the new neoliberal-authoritarian coalition that was less interested in democratic procedures than what its members perceived as the survival of the existing order. If the Peruvian experience is not easily repeatable, it should nonetheless stand as an example of the dangers accompanying economic reform and democratization in a context of the state's institutional fragmentation and inefficacy.

Notes

1. This chapter appeared as part of the article "State Reform, Coalitions, and the Neoliberal Autogolpe in Peru," *Latin American Research Review* 30:1, 1995, pp. 7–37. Reprinted with permission.

2. Press reports emphasized Fujimori's speeches against the upper class and suggested he would call for a multi-party government. See *La República* (Dominical), April 15, 1990, p. 1; and *La República*, April 2, 1990, p. 9.

3. A rundown on some key advisors is provided in *Caretas*, February 4, 1991, pp. 34–36. On the importance of De Soto in the "reinsertion" program and anti-drug policy see *Caretas*, February 3, 1992, pp. 10–14. Even though De Soto resigned as Fujimori's drug czar, his influence continued to be felt. In the debates regarding changes in the electoral system, De Soto's proposals for new electoral districts received widespread publicity and a sympathetic hearing from the regime. *El Comercio*, July 14, 1992, p. A4.

4. See in particular the special report in *Caretas*, June 3, 1991, pp. 1–16; and Ariela Ruíz Caro, "Reinserción: Cuentas de Nunca Acabar," *QueHacer* 73, September 1990, pp. 12–17.

5. *Caretas*, December 2, 1991, p. 29.

6. Reports on Montesinos have been extensive, although this mysterious figure has never given a formal interview. See for example *Caretas*, June 10, 1991, pp. 19–22; and "Peru Adviser Linked to Drug Cartels," *Miami Herald*, April 18, 1992. p. 1. Secretive presidential advisors are not without precedents in recent Latin American politics. In Argentina, José López Rega, with his proclivities for the occult and right-wing paramilitary politics, exercised a Rasputin-like influence over Isabel Perón during her ill-fated tenure.

7. The call by a group of retired military officials for a civil-military "co-government" in early 1991 fueled much of this speculation and may in retrospect have been a trial balloon. See *Sí*, March 25, 1991, pp. 17–19.

8. For a summary of electoral results see Fernando Tuesta, *Peru Político en Cifras* (Lima: Friedrich Ebert, 1987). For a broad discussion of electoral trends also see Maxwell Cameron, *Democracy and Authoritarianism in Peru* (New York: St. Martins, 1994).

9. This problem of "representation" is one that the parties themselves have acknowledged, especially in leftist circles. In 1989, the IU held its first national congress, and made several attempts to create a unified, elected structure. Party leaders, however, vetoed most attempts to change the collegial governance of the front, thus allowing the leaders themselves to decide the coalition's policies. Clearly, traditional parties showed little ability to rejuvenate their leaderships or introduce internal democracy, outcomes that contributed to the stunning success of independents after 1989.

10. Much of the lead that Vargas Llosa enjoyed during the 1990 campaign was based upon his image as an outsider. But his long and exhaustive campaign during the eighteen months prior to the election made him a familiar figure to most voters by election day. Moreover, the growing visibility of traditional politicians from Acción Popular and the Partido Popular Cristiano, who were members

of Vargas Llosa's alliance FREDEMO, convinced many that behind Vargas lay the same old faces. On the election see especially, C.I. Degregori and R. Grompone, *Elecciones 1990: Demonios y Redentores en el Nuevo Perú* (Lima: Instituto de Estudios Peruanos, 1991).

11. The divisions among the parties of the right were strongest in Vargas Llosa's own Movimiento Libertad. One-third of Libertad's congresional delegation resigned to openly support Fujimori's administration. Mario Vargas Llosa, *El Pez en el Agua: Memorias* (Barcelona: Seix Barral, 1993), p. 35.

12. A poll of Lima residents found that 40 percent could not identify a single leader of the opposition to Fujimori. The person named most often (by 12 percent of the respondents) as leader of the opposition, Fernando Olivera, consistently backed the regime. Alberto Adrianzen, "Y la Opposicion, Donde Esta?" *QueHacer* 70, March 1991, pp. 10–13.

13. The most notable case was that of leftist economist Carlos Amat y Leon. Appointed by Fujimori as minister of agriculture, Amat soon found himself undercut by the neoliberal Prime Minister Juan Hurtado Miller.

14. A comprehensive review of the decrees can be found in *Actualidad Económico* 129, November 1991, p. 6; and *Latin American Weekly Report*, WR-91-46, November 28, 1991, pp. 2–3.

15. On the expanded role of the SIN see *Sí*, November 25, 1991, pp. 26–27. An unprecedented public view of the spy agency is offered in an interview with General Edwin Díaz, former director of the SIN in *Caretas*, January 21, 1993, pp. 28–29. Unsurprisingly, Díaz denied any involvement in telephone espionage. The role of the SIN in influencing reporting of the November 1992 military rebellion is documented extensively in *Caretas*, December 3, 1992, pp. 18–19.

16. See Chapter Eight for an expanded discussion.

17. On the virtual dismantlement of development banks, such as Banco Minero, see Germán Alarcón, "Modernización o Retroceso?" *QueHacer* 74, November 1991, pp. 14–15. On the agrarian sector see *Caretas*, April 8, 1991, pp. 26–29.

18. *Sí*, July 27, 1992, p. 24.

19. As with other neoliberal regimes, Fujimori uses the term "labor flexibility" to describe the reforms being introduced. Since the *autogolpe*, changes have been largely introduced by decree. See *Caretas*, December 10, 1992, pp. 24–25. On the changes enacted before April 1992 and their effects on labor organization see *Caretas*, October 21, 1991, p. 22.

20. See especially, Eliana Chávez, "El Empleo en los Sectores Populares Urbanos" in Alberto Bustamante, ed., *De Marginales a Informales* (Lima: DESCO, 1990), pp. 73–124.

21. *La República*, October 9, 1990, p. 10; *Sí*, December 23, 1991, pp. 18–20; *La República*, March 17, 1991, pp. 7–9.

22. On Fujimori's attacks see *Caretas*, December 16, 1991, p. 11.

23. *Sí*, January 6, 1992, p. 8.

24. Many Fujimori supporters pointed to Yeltsin's forcible closing of the Russian Parliament, and the US support for that action, in October 1993 to assert the legitimacy of Fujimori's autogolpe. There are, however, significant differences between the two moves. Yeltsin's actions came in the midst of an incomplete tran-

sition from totalitarian institutions, where democratic institutions had not yet been formed and much of the opposition had strong authoritarian tendencies. None of these conditions applied to Peru prior to April 1992.

25. The *"Fujigolpe"* came on the heels of an attempted coup in Venezuela in February 1992 against President Carlos Andrés Pérez and the September 1991 overthrow of President Jean Bertrand Aristide in Haiti. These events led many to speculate about a new authoritarian wave in Latin America. An authoritarian outcome was similarly feared in Eastern Europe, where battles between the executive and legislative powers could provoke a breakdown. On the immediate ramifications of the *Fujigolpe* and the perspective of the Bush administration see Thomas Friedman, "Peru and US: What Course to Take?" *New York Times,* April 15, 1992, p. 3.

26. *Caretas,* May 10, 1993, pp. 10–16.

27. This point is made especially clear in Guillermo O'Donnell, Philippe Schmitter, and Laurence Whitehead, eds., *Transitions From Authoritarian Rule: Tentative Conclusions About Uncertain Outcomes* (Baltimore: Johns Hopkins University Press, 1986), p. 15.

28. José María Salcedo, *Terremoto: Cómo y Pórque Ganó Fujimori* (Lima: Ediciones Brasa, 1995).

PART TWO

State Power and Social Control

6

Villa El Salvador:
Popular Organization
and the State in a Lima Shantytown

Since the 1950s the coastal desert fringes to the north and south of Lima were the main areas of settlement for migrants to the city. Amid the large sand dunes and rocky hills, migrants from the Andean provinces of the highlands established their precarious dwellings. One of the largest "invasions" of migrants occurred in April 1971, 20 kilometers south of downtown Lima on the desert plain, Tablada de Lurín. Known as Villa El Salvador, the area has since become one of the largest shantytown districts in Lima. It is the seventh largest district in Lima, and on its own would represent the sixth largest city in Peru. It also has been one of the most politically organized. The unique organizational scheme developed in Villa under the Velasco regime flourished long after the end of that regime and was expanded as new social organizations developed to meet the needs and demands of its growing population.

This chapter will examine the relation between political organizations among the popular sector residents of Villa El Salvador and the state. Villa's evolution from a corporatist experiment to a bastion of grassroots organization provides important insights into the limits of state power in society. The first part of this chapter examines the development of Villa in light of changing state-society relations. Those relations should not be seen as zero-sum. State intervention in Villa in the early 1970s resulted in significant organizational opportunities for social actors. The system of corporatist neighborhood representation (Comunidad Urbana Autogestionaria de Villa El Salvador, CUAVES) designed "from above" during the Velasco regime created an important political space for resident participation. By the end of the 1980s, Villa had developed a complex societal network that effectively limited state prerogatives.

The second part of the chapter examines the relation between self-management in the district and the role of state institutions. Grassroots organizations not only became the main governing institutions in Villa El Salvador, but in areas such as urban planning, economic development, and education, limited state intervention into local affairs. In the process, Villa became a symbol and model of governance where *"autogestión"* (self-management) predominated over the traditional methods of local governance, including partisan clientelism and centralized bureaucratic planning. The model of *autogestión* introduced by SINAMOS and based on Yugoslav models of management, not only survived, but was adopted by the United Left (IU) as one of their ideological banners. As applied in Villa, *autogestión* meant that residents decided neighborhood policies through their participation on a series of regularly elected local committees.

By the late 1980s Villa had acquired an important status among Lima's poor districts. Its model of organization was internationally recognized. Socialist leaders such as Willy Brandt, Julius Nyerere, and Carlos Andrés Pérez visited the district, along with Pope John Paul II. In 1988 the United Nations designated the district a "messenger of peace" and district leaders received Spain's prestigious "Premio Príncipe de Asturias" in recognition of the district's contribution to peace. Nonetheless, Villa did not escape the economic crisis and violence affecting the rest of the country. Both Sendero Luminoso and the military came to view community leaders as potential enemies. Moreover, the organizational structure of Villa was repeatedly challenged by the Fujimori regime and the Mayor of Lima during the early 1990s, Ricardo Belmont. Both felt politically threatened by the radical independence of the district.

Aside from its unique organizational structure, Villa El Salvador is a typical shantytown district suffering from the same problems of other poor districts in Lima. According to a mid-1980s census, Villa's population is characterized by its extreme poverty, relative youth, and precarious health. Of the district's 250,000 residents, 52 percent were under eighteen years of age and 40 percent were twelve or under. Among the economically active population, instability predominated. Only 38 percent of the district's economically active population was adequately employed. Most of the population was either underemployed (46 percent) or unemployed (16 percent) and as a result received less than the minimum wage. One of the clearest signs of poverty was the high infant mortality rate, which was above the average for metropolitan Lima. In addition, an estimated 43 percent of infants born in the district demonstrated some sign of malnutrition.[1]

From Corporatist Experiment to Socialist Utopia

The Model Shantytown: 1971–1976

The invasion that led to the creation of Villa El Salvador exposed the ambiguities of the Velasco regime's mobilization project.[2] How could a "revolutionary" government bent on gaining popular support for the reforms being carried out repress a group of humble citizens who had invaded a desert strip to set up their homes? The initial response to the invasion, directed by the law and order oriented Minister of Interior General Armando Artola Azcarate, dramatized this situation. Artola ordered the police to dislodge all invaders, a task which was violent (several dead and over fifty injured) as well as unsuccessful. Invaders fought with the police, retreated, and when the police left, returned to occupy their terrain. The most difficult confrontation, however, came not with the land invaders but with Church leaders who worked in shantytowns (called *pueblos jóvenes*, or young towns) and saw the invasion as a just solution to their housing needs. The most prominent Church representative in this matter was Monseñor Luis Bambarén whose work among shantytown dwellers had earned him the name of "Bishop of the Pueblos Jóvenes." Several days after the first violent confrontation between the police and the invaders, Bambarén visited Villa and declared that residents had a right to establish their homes with dignity and without repression. In response, General Artola ordered Bambarén's imprisonment on charges of "agitation." The protest from the Church and most political sectors was swift and led to the immediate release of Bambarén and the resignation of Artola on orders from General Velasco. The politics of state repression had failed and the politics of state cooptation was to begin.

On May 12, 1971, only fourteen days after the initial invasion began, army trucks transported those interested in settling in Villa El Salvador. Villa was to be transformed from a regime embarrassment to a model of the benefits of the revolution. As events unfolded, it was apparent that the regime had no plans in the wings to deal with this situation. Thus, the military's policy toward Villa developed slowly, responding as much to pressure "from below" as it did to the conflicting goals of the regime's mobilization project.

One of the first initiatives undertaken by the regime involved the physical design of the district. The Oficina Nacional de Pueblos Jóvenes (ONDEPJOV), created in 1968, was charged with planning the allocation of land to provide for its rational usage and to avoid the chaos of other shantytown districts. The scheme was a paragon of military orderliness. Villa was divided into five sectors, each composed of twenty-four residential groups. In turn, each residential group was made up of sixteen blocks that were composed of twenty-four lots measuring 140 square meters. Land was also set aside for industry, agriculture, and recreation.[3] Little was left to chance. Land conflicts, common in most shantytowns, were resolved by an equitable arrangement that assigned all residents an equal lot.

The demands of residents appeared, however, to outpace the capacity of the regime's planning. By July 1971 the first resident organizations were formed to pressure authorities to provide a school in the shanty-town. Soon, neighborhood juntas were set up. From the beginning, com-munity leaders organized residents around demands for basic services. One leader of the period, Antonio Aragón, noted that their strategy was "demand and carry out" because "the government was unable to resolve all of our problems by themselves." A key aspect behind this strategy, according to Aragón, was the importance of labor union experience for local leaders. Key leaders during this initial phase, including Aragón, Apolinario Rojas, and Odilón Mucha, had been active union members or leaders of New Left parties with a strong *clasista* union agenda. Meetings, rallies, and assemblies were all practices then being developed among the new *clasista* unions linked to Maoists or the Communist Party and also applied by Villa's leaders to the problems of the new shantytown.[4]

In early 1972 the regime handed over responsibility for neighborhood organizations in Villa to SINAMOS. SINAMOS was to regulate and dis-tribute resources as well as to provide advice. The relationship that devel-oped between local leaders and SINAMOS was complex. Although pro-regime leaders dominated Villa's organizations, this did not mean that SINAMOS imposed its will. Local leaders had ample autonomy and were responsible to their neighborhood junta, where they were elected, and not to SINAMOS. Moreover, the conflicts and contradictions in the regime made a consistent and unified policy virtually impossible, either through SINAMOS or other channels. As we saw in Chapter Two, infighting and contradictory goals were reaching a high point in the regime during this period. Local leaders, influenced by the regime's most radical rhetoric, were well aware of these differences and sought out those officials most sympathetic to their demands. As Aragón pointed out,

> The structure of General Velasco's government was not homogeneous. There were functionaries and ministers who had nationalistic, progressive and socializing ideas and those who had reactionary notions, and we in Villa El Salvador had to maneuver in these waters and know how to achieve concrete objectives for the good of our community.[5]

The autonomy of local leaders was demonstrated during the creation of CUAVES, the main decision-making body in the shantytown. One of the first steps SINAMOS took was to call for all existing leaders of neighborhood juntas to resign in preparation for new elections. Each residential group was to have a duly elected secretary general at the head of its junta. By the end of 1972 a group of residential leaders took the initiative to organize a convention of neighborhood organizations to consolidate the developing system. Following a meeting with SINAMOS officials, where the idea was approved, an organizing committee was formed.[6] The I Congress of Delegates of Villa El Salvador was held in late July 1973 with nearly 700 delegates participating from different neighborhood organizations. As a show of support for this congress, two of the regime's leading progressive officers—Generals Fernández Maldonado and Rodriguez Figueroa—participated as observers.

The convention lasted three days and was filled with lively debates dominated by radical rhetoric and resolutions. One resolution included in the final political document declared:

> The people of Villa El Salvador reject, condemn and repudiate all social, political, and cultural organization, based on the capitalist system and incorporate into our community, our social conduct, our neighborhood organization, and our economic, political and cultural creations, the socialist principals of solidarity and fraternity among peoples.[7]

The statement stood in sharp contrast to the usual political declarations of the Velasco regime, fraught with ideological ambiguity about "neither communism nor capitalism." The most important result of this convention, however, was the effort to institutionalize Villa's system of neighborhood organization. The system known as the Comunidad Urbana Autogestionaria de Villa El Salvador (CUAVES) was to be the main decision-making body in the shantytown, representing all residents on the basis of the physical division of Villa.

The organization of the CUAVES encompassed virtually every aspect of neighborhood life, from the block level up. Its structure and functions remained in place over the following two decades, even as the country's political system was convulsed by major crises. The 108 residential groups of Villa all have the same structure. Each block is directed by a block committee composed of functional secretariats (health, education, security, recreation). All sixteen blocks of a residential group elect members to a central junta, composed of a secretary general, sub-secretary general, and functional secretariats responsible for their residential group.[8] In addition, each residential group has a general assembly which

meets regularly so residents can air their demands and meet with their local junta.

Every two years, the 108 juntas of Villa meet in a convention and elect an executive council (*consejo ejecutivo comunal*, CEC) led by a secretary general. The eleven member CEC is the primary governing and coordinating council of the CUAVES, and its secretary general is the official leader of the CUAVES. All major decisions which affected Villa El Salvador, including its relations with the central government, the municipality, non-governmental organizations, and private firms, have traditionally been made by this council.

An important element included in the design of the CUAVES was the prohibition on reelection. This provision was designed to allow the widest possible participation of residents in the system and to prevent the development of personal cliques that might perpetuate themselves in power. All residents could, therefore, have an opportunity to participate in the CUAVES. As a result of the no reelection clause in the CUAVES statutes, "all residents have been, or have had in their families, at least one neighborhood leader."[9]

The CUAVES began to function in late 1973, just as the infighting in the Velasco regime began to intensify. By early 1974 progressive officers in the regime were losing their influence to "*La Misión*," while SINAMOS reoriented its activity away from participationist experiments. The increased conflicts were felt in Villa and the CUAVES. New Left parties, especially the Maoist Patria Roja which had a strong local presence through the teachers union, increasingly attacked CUAVES leaders for their ties to the military. Their criticisms received a sympathetic hearing from residents frustrated by their lack of basic services in the shantytown.

In September 1975, just a few days after the overthrow of General Velasco by Morales Bermúdez, the II CUAVES Convention was held. The convention was dominated by a fierce ideological battle among pro-regime forces (over support of the coup and the role of SINAMOS) and between these forces and a radical group led by Patria Roja.[10] After the II Convention, state officials distanced themselves from the CUAVES and adopted an openly hostile attitude toward its leadership. SINAMOS withdrew its support from Villa, which no longer received favorable treatment from government ministries. In turn, the new CUAVES leadership—a mix of radical *velasquistas* and Maoists led by Patria's Odilón Mucha as secretary general—declared their opposition to the Morales regime and urged increased ties with other opposition groups on the left.

Confrontation and Continuity: 1976–1982

Throughout the late 1970s, the CUAVES, like other popular sector organizations around the country, protested Morales' program of economic austerity through rallies, marches, demonstrations, and hunger strikes. In April 1976 the CUAVES organized one of the largest protests in Lima. With most institutional channels turning a deaf ear on their demands for increased services, the CUAVES held a massive march of 20,000 residents from Villa to the presidential palace in the center of Lima. The march included prominent labor and New Left party leaders who demonstrated in solidarity with residents. Mucha and other CUAVES leaders were received by a surprised Morales Bermúdez, who promised that their demands would get a fair hearing.[11] Yet events soon took a turn for the worst when the regime unleashed the first of a series of economic austerity packages and cracked down on opposition groups. In late July, Mucha and most of the CUAVES CEC were jailed.

Despite this repression, CUAVES leaders continued their opposition activities against the regime. Military repression against the CUAVES and other popular sector organizations did not result in the disbanding of these structures which remained intact, albeit with new or temporary leaders, and served as important political spaces to express opposition to the regime. Through 1978 the CUAVES organized a number of protests, including solidarity strikes with the teachers union, SUTEP, and violent demonstrations during the national strikes of July 1977 and May 1978.

Opposition to the Morales regime did not, however, end the political divisions that affected Villa from the start. As leftist groups throughout the country moved toward greater unity in the late 1970s, the left in Villa remained divided. Neither Patria nor the radical *velasquistas*, grouped in a small local faction (MRS) without a base beyond Villa, participated in the constituent assembly elections. Both groups, therefore, remained marginalized from the growing imperative in the left to join forces at a national level.

The isolation of Villa's leadership from national trends could not last long. The return to electoral democracy in 1980, with freely elected municipal governments, posed a new challenge to Villa El Salvador by bringing into question the need for a system of representation parallel to that of elected municipal authorities. As a result of various decrees passed by Morales and strengthened by the new Belaúnde regime, jurisdiction and administration in shantytowns passed from the central government to local municipalities. Villa thus found itself just one more shantytown within the municipal district of Villa María de Triunfo.

The Acción Popular controlled municipality of Villa María refused to deal directly with the CUAVES, arguing that the CUAVES was not legally constituted and lacked representation. The new municipal government was openly hostile to Villa El Salvador, which already had a reputation as a "communist" neighborhood. Villa found itself designated a low priority zone where basic services, especially garbage collection, were reduced. In

February 1982, in a clear attempt to eliminate the CUAVES, the municipal government of Lima passed a resolution requiring all existing neighborhood organizations to reconstitute themselves as "neighborhood associations."[12] Unlike the CUAVES, these neighborhood associations lacked the authority to make or implement their own policies. In a unanimous fashion, the CUAVES voted to reject that resolution and simply refused to recognize its validity.

The difficulties posed by the return to elected municipal governments and a growing consensus that the Patria-MSR feud had paralyzed the CUAVES and turned it into a fiefdom of factional interests, led to the creation in June 1982 of a commission to study how Villa could reinvigorate its organizations. Led by Michel Azcueta, a Spanish-born teacher who worked in the first school set up by the Church in Villa, the Colegio Fe y Alegría, Azcueta had numerous connections to parochial groups throughout the community. The strong presence of Catholic lay workers among the "renovation" movement in Villa, and more specifically of Catholic lay groups inspired by the "liberation theology" of Peru's Gustavo Gutíerrez, highlighted the important role of the Church.

The first group of Catholic lay workers arrived in Villa with the initial invasion. The outspokenness of Monseñor Bambarén and his jailing were only the most visible signs of support for the invasion offered by progressive sectors of the Church. Lay workers spearheaded the effort to build a school system in Villa. The first school was the Jesuit-run Fe y Alegría, designed to teach communal values and identities as well as to contribute to the formation of community leaders. Along with schools, these workers also built a theater school and mothers club. In all of these projects, it was lay workers and base communities (CEB's) organized around local parishes rather than the "official" Church hierarchy that took the initiative. Church workers generally concentrated their organizational enthusiasm on projects that did not impinge upon the prerogatives of either the military regime or the CUAVES, thus avoiding serious disputes with both political authorities and the Church hierarchy. This strategy of avoiding conflict paralleled that followed by the progressive Church elsewhere in Peru.[13]

In mid-1982, the Azcueta Commission proposed turning Villa El Salvador into a municipal district, thus eliminating the growing political isolation of Villa and the conflicts with the municipality of Villa María. With the support of IU and APRA, the commission's recommendation was taken to the congress, where the creation of municipalities had to be approved. Despite municipal opposition from Villa María, in May 1983 the congress passed a resolution creating the new municipal district of Villa El Salvador.

The transformation of Villa from a shantytown into a municipal district had important political implications. First, it represented the consolidation of Villa and its peculiar system of governance. As a municipal district, political authorities in Villa lessened their dependence upon external political officials from the Lima municipality and the central government. The role of the CUAVES system, which had existed in legal limbo since 1980, would now be legally determined by the district's residents through their municipal government, since district governments were charged with overseeing neighborhood associations. On paper at least, the existence of the CUAVES no longer appeared necessary once Villa became a municipality, with its own budget, elected officials, and social services. Yet the issue of the need for the CUAVES never even arose among local leaders. In practice, the CUAVES was intimately linked to Villa's identity, symbolizing what was "special" about Villa: a model of self-government outside of the formal-legal political structure. Nonetheless, the municipal-CUAVES relation posed serious questions regarding local governance.

The municipal-CUAVES relation was only possible due to the important shift in partisan dynamics in Villa. For the first time since the I CUAVES Convention in 1973, a single political force dominated Villa El Salvador—the United Left. In the municipal elections of 1983, IU's Michel Azcueta was elected the new district's first mayor and IU controlled both the municipality and the CUAVES.

The Municipal Experience, 1984–1989

During its first six years as a municipal district, the United Left consistently dominated all of the elected positions in the district at the municipal level and in the CUAVES. This was not surprising insofar as leftist political parties were the only political actors in Villa since the early 1970s. None of the traditional parties (APRA, AP or PPC) attempted to organize residents around an alternative set of political demands or issues, nor did they dispute the left's political hegemony. By contrast, a leftist discourse had been part of Villa's political existence from the beginning, first through the military regime and SINAMOS and than through Maoist and *velasquista* parties. The entire conception of the CUAVES that gave Villa its distinct identity, had arisen from that discourse.

One of the first problems facing the new mayor of Villa El Salvador was the relationship with the CUAVES. According to its statutes, the CUAVES was the supreme governing institution in Villa El Salvador. This created a clear conflict with the new district municipality that shared a similar status under the 1979 Constitution. Which would be the primary governing institution in Villa—the municipality or the CUAVES? In January 1984 leaders of the CUAVES and the new municipal council led by Azcueta met in Villa's communal pharmacy (Sector 2, Group 4, block N) to negotiate a formal agreement outlining the terms of their relation. Despite the apparent conflict of powers, the role of the CUAVES was not at issue. From the beginning, Azcueta conceded that the CUAVES was the most representative institution in Villa, and as such the backbone of the district.[14]

With that point agreed upon from the start, the main task was to delineate responsibilities. A compromise signed at the end of the month adopted a solomonic approach to this problem.[15] The mayor officially recognized and promised to respect the CUAVES system and its statutes as the "only instrument that governs communal life." The CUAVES was also given the authority to decide, in coordination with the municipality, questions involving housing, education, health, markets, and communal enterprises. However, the CUAVES somewhat ambiguously recognized the mayor's authority "over the entire district." Both sides committed themselves to coordinate their activities "fraternally" and, in the event of disagreements, to use the general assembly of the CUAVES as final arbiter.

The agreement between municipal authorities and the CUAVES outlined a relationship that was virtually outside the sphere of existing formal-legal political structures in Peru. There was no legal basis, and none was sought, for ceding what was the governing power of the municipality to a neighborhood organization such as the CUAVES. Moreover, the entire arrangement was designed and carried out by local Villa authorities without any role for officials of either the central government or the municipal government of Lima. The state, as such, was completely absent from this informal agreement. In effect, the formal structures of the state took a back seat to the CUAVES. The system of representation and elections implicit in the formal-legal system were deemed insufficient by the leaders of Villa and secondary to the system of political participation and self-government already practiced in the CUAVES. The accord between the CUAVES and municipal candidates in 1986 illustrated the degree to which the CUAVES had substituted formal structures. All candidates promised to respect the primacy of the CUAVES and reduced the municipality to little more than a municipal commission.

With the understanding that the electoral process is a constitutional formality, we recognize that the CUAVES is a representative organism of historical popular sovereignty and of communal self-government, for which we clearly express that ... our task as mayor or councilmen is a task charged by our community, that is to say, it is a municipal commission under the supreme authority of our general assemblies.[16]

The informality that characterized the relation between the CUAVES and the municipality had an important impact upon the day-to-day functioning of the district. The budgetary process highlights this dynamic. The district of Villa El Salvador, in accordance with municipal regulations, had its own budget. Funds were received from the central government, the municipality of Lima, and local fees and taxes. In the case of Villa, however, the municipal budget was shared with the CUAVES. The municipality transferred funds to the CUAVES and allowed the CUAVES to impose fees and taxes in the district. Both the transfer of funds and the imposition of taxes by the CUAVES were technically illegal, yet they ensured the survival of the municipal-CUAVES relationship.[17]

The consensus that existed in Villa over the rules that governed the administration of the district did not, however, eliminate political differences or conflicts. During the García administration the governing APRA party used state resources to intervene in Villa. The social policies adopted by the APRA government and the APRA-led Lima municipality elected in 1986, were implemented in a highly partisan fashion. Housing and employment programs developed to improve living conditions in shantytowns were soon converted into the sort of clientelism APRA practiced during its sixty year history.[18] One of the social programs designed by the central government as the centerpiece of its shantytown policy was the PAIT, a temporary employment program introduced in October 1985. Workers contracted under PAIT were assigned to municipal tasks such as park maintenance and garbage collection. From the start, the program appeared to be designed with political rather than technical criteria. PAIT was administered directly from the presidential palace through Cooperación Popular, a development agency founded in the 1960s.

PAIT administrators left little doubt that the most important criteria to be eligible for employment in PAIT was support for APRA. PAIT workers were told to mark the APRA star in the November 1986 municipal elections "because that is what gives us work."[19] Few efforts were made to dissimulate the political character of PAIT employment. Many residents in Villa El Salvador recall the "work" carried out by PAIT laborers in 1986 on a sand hill off the PanAmerican Highway. PAIT workers spent weeks collecting large white stones throughout the district and than gathered them at the hill. Within several days those stones had been arranged on the hill to form a series of letters that could be seen from most of Villa: ALAN=PAIT.

APRA's efforts to establish a clientelist base in shantytowns through its use of state resources brought it into open conflict with IU, which had established a presence in these areas already. One study concluded that the best explanation for the distribution of PAIT jobs among the poor districts of Lima was the vote received by IU in previous elections, not the level of unemployment, income, or relative poverty of the district.[20]

The hostility of the APRA regime toward Villa was expressed in a variety of ways, from cuts in funding to efforts to circumvent municipal and CUAVES authorities when implementing development projects. Despite these pressures, the CUAVES demonstrated its control of district politics and a high degree of autonomy in its relation toward the state. The organizational power of CUAVES guaranteed that autonomy: all decisions affecting the district had to be approved by the CUAVES CEC or the General Assembly. The multiple layers of authority, from the block level to the General Assembly, made it difficult for any one actor to impose its will on the entire district. The PAIT, which was the most extensive effort by APRA to set up a clientelist network in Villa, was developed outside of the CUAVES structure, and thus attempted to get around the institutional rules which governed the district.[21] However, by operating outside the CUAVES system, PAIT lost any influence it might have gained had it been incorporated into CUAVES. PAIT's influence was therefore restricted to its capacity to provide jobs. As that capacity decreased with the economic recession in 1988, so did the political loyalties acquired. By late 1989, the number of jobs PAIT provided in the district was only a quarter of those provided in 1986, and the program was later terminated by the Fujimori administration. Thus, despite APRA's attempt to make partisan inroads into Villa El Salvador, the district remained a bastion of IU during the 1980s.

New Social Movements and the State

Throughout the mid to late 1980s, a series of new social and political organizations were founded in Villa. These organizations included a women's association, popular kitchens, *vaso de leche* (glass of milk) committees, a small business association, and popular libraries. Together, they added a new layer of complexity to Villa's web of social relations. Like new social movements elsewhere in Latin America, most of these groups organized around gender, family and cultural issues, making them more than class- oriented organizations.[22] Although the initiative to form these groups came from different actors, they all attempted to alleviate the economic problems facing residents during the recession of the 1980s. Throughout the shantytowns of Lima, residents found that they could only survive economically and acquire a political voice by pooling their meager resources.

The glass of milk program in Villa El Salvador illustrates the complexity of popular organization and their relation to the state. Political parties, the Church, CUAVES, the women's association (Federación Popular de Mujeres de Villa El Salvador, FEPOMUVES), non-governmental organizations (NGOs), and the municipalities (both Villa and Lima), had an important role in the functioning of this program. The numerous groups and institutions involved at different levels of the program's organization tended to hinder wide scale clientelism. Participation in the program reenforced political identification with a radical leftist discourse and particularly with the IU. The program provided substantial benefits to residents by helping meet basic needs that otherwise would go unattended.

Both the glass of milk committees and popular kitchens arose to meet a key problem among the urban lower-class: malnutrition and infant mortality. Popular kitchens began to appear in the late 1970s and laid the basis for the glass of milk program. As we saw in Chapter Three, the first kitchens were set up in the local parishes of popular districts, usually through the parish mothers club. The Church played a key role in the initial organization of the kitchens. Not only did parishes serve as a locale for kitchen committees, but Catholic lay groups and NGO's provided the technical assistance needed to make the kitchens function, from organizational training to arranging the donations of stoves and food. Foodstuffs were bought wholesale at low cost and supplemented by donations from international organizations, primarily CARITAS. The kitchens were organized according to the *autogestión* model. Each kitchen had a directorate that included a coordinator, a secretary of correspondence, a secretary of economy, a secretary of security, and a secretary of warehousing. The directorate was elected on a yearly basis in a general assembly of all the members of a kitchen, that included up to one hundred residents. Election regulations were strict: kitchen leaders could not be members of the same family, could not be reelected more than once, and could not occupy a leadership position in any other district organization. These rules were designed to avoid the development of cliques or clientelist practices. According to one commonly used organizational manual, candidates had to demonstrate a democratic character, responsibility, and honorability.[23] The kitchens were urged to promote communitarian, participatory, and democratic values.

To what extent were those goals of democratic participation and communalism achieved? The experience during the 1980s in Villa suggested that the kitchens largely avoided becoming clientelist mechanisms for outside agents. This was in part the result of their autonomy vis-à-vis the state and political parties. The kitchens emerged "from below" and depended on Church groups and NGOs for their initial organization and resources. Neither the state nor political parties had an established institutional role in the program or participated as such in the designation of tasks, funds, or leaders. Their lack of direct control over resources and the participatory character of the kitchens reduced the possibility of clientelist manipulation.

The experience of the kitchens led to the more extensive glass of milk program, begun in 1983 by IU's Mayor Alfonso Barrantes to ensure every child in the city at least one glass of milk a day. Barrantes began the program by soliciting donations of milk from the European Economic Community. The donations were the only source of milk for the program during its first six months. In the following period, the congress approved special funding to buy milk domestically in Peru, supplementing the donations received from abroad. Unlike the kitchen program, the glass of milk program was from the start an initiative "from above" and depended for resources on the municipality of Lima. The program was designed, however, to specifically avoid clientelism through the creation of the same sorts of multiple levels of authority and local elections that existed on the kitchen committee.[24] Although the program underwent a variety of changes during the García and Fujimori regimes, the basic structure remained intact through the early 1990s.

In Villa El Salvador, the glass of milk program was carried out in coordination with the CUAVES, thereby overlapping with the spatial division that governed the CUAVES system. Thus, each residential group had a glass of milk committee (CVL), with a president, health secretary, and social assistant. One of the effects of the kitchens and glass of milk programs was to increase the salience of gender politics in the district. In both organizations, women were the main protagonists, accounting for the vast majority of organizers and beneficiaries. The first strictly women's organization was the FEPOMUVES.[25] Founded in 1983, it soon became an arena where women from the kitchen committees and the glass of milk program discussed their problems and shared information.

After March 1987, the FEPOMUVES was given the authority to distribute the milk arriving from the Lima municipality. Under the previous system, the milk that arrived at the Villa municipality was warehoused and distributed by a municipal glass of milk committee. Under the new system, milk from Lima's municipality was received by representatives from FEPOMUVES who stored it in eight centers throughout Villa. At those centers, representatives from the 108 residential group CVL's arrived every few days to receive their quota of milk, that they in turn distributed to their group.

By giving FEPOMUVES this function, the municipality effectively abdicated part of its authority. The role of FEPOMUVES in the distribution of milk occurred outside the norms that governed the program in the rest of the city. The accord signed between FEPOMUVES and the municipality of Villa was an informal arrangement granting authority to the women's organization to administer the program in the district. Despite the fact that program designers did not include a role for outside agents such as FEPOMUVES in the program and that the municipality did not have the legal authority to transfer the distribution of milk to FEPOMUVES, the program functioned under this informal arrangement until challenged by the Fujimori administration. As with other aspects of Villa's governance, such as the CUAVES-municipality relationship, the role of FEPOMUVES in the glass of milk program illustrates how the district was governed by rules worked out informally among local actors rather than by arrangements designed by the state.

The glass of milk program, like the popular kitchens, represented an important experience in organization and participation for those involved. Politically, both programs were closely identified with the United Left, which funded and organized these programs through its municipal government in Lima (1983–1986) and its control of Villa's municipality (1983–1993). As a result of these partisan ties, the programs incurred the hostility of other political groups. Both programs faced repeated challenges by the APRA mayor of Lima, Jorge Del Castillo (1986–1989); his successor, the "independent" mayor Ricardo Belmont (1989–1995); and by the Fujimori administration. Despite these difficulties, the glass of milk and popular kitchen programs filled an important nutritional need among the urban poor that would have otherwise gone unattended.

Conclusion

Villa El Salvador was a creation of Velasco's developmentalist state. Few state interventions in recent Peruvian history were more ambitious than the creation and organization of Villa. Not only did the state encourage settlement in Villa, but it also created a system of self-government as a model for other shantytowns. Yet the state's attempt to reshape society in Villa and in other urban shantytowns, was short-lived. With the downfall of Velasco, the role of the state changed dramatically. Support for the district was withdrawn, demands for services were left unaddressed, and the state made its presence felt only through occasional repression. By 1983, when the shantytown was converted into a municipal district, the state had seemingly withdrawn from attempts to influence popular urban districts.

The reduced presence of the state in Villa and the development of CUAVES allowed the district to develop informally, according to rules set by local authorities that often contradicted or violated the state's formal procedures. The model of self-government that predominated in Villa created an important opportunity to fill the vacuum left by a highly limited state presence. Through the early 1990s, the CUAVES maintained jurisdiction over virtually all aspects of neighborhood life, acting as the primary governing body in Villa El Salvador. Both the CUAVES-municipality and FEPOMUVES-glass of milk relationships illustrate the degree to which informal arrangements created by local actors predominated over formal rules set by the state. In both instances, the CUAVES set the norms that governed these relationships and technically violated bureaucratic procedures set forth by the state. Despite the irregularity of these arrangements, local actors accepted them because of the CUAVES' legitimacy as the primary governing body in Villa and the perception that they served the interests of the district.

As political polarization and violence increased dramatically in the country, Villa did not escape its effects. The violent campaign Sendero Luminoso initiated was also felt in the district. In late 1988 Sendero began to threaten local leaders, warning that their participation in the CUAVES amounted to cooperation with "revisionists." The Mayor of Villa El Salvador, Michel Azcueta, received numerous death threats from Sendero and survived a nearly fatal assassination attempt. In February 1992, the lieutenant mayor of Villa and head of FEPOMUVES, María Elena Moyano, was assassinated by Sendero. The violence even reached the level of the popular kitchens where women were warned not to participate and several were attacked and killed. Military forces, the police, and paramilitary organizations also viewed those participating in local activities with suspicion and labeled all who might challenge the state's authority as subversive. Increasingly, participating in neighborhood organizations meant risking one's life. For Sendero, participation in any organization that did not contribute to its revolution amounted to cooperating with its enemies. Villa's residents, like the poor elsewhere in Peru, were thus caught in the crossfire of escalating violence.

Notes

1. Comunidad Urbana Autogestionaria de Villa El Salvador, *Villa El Salvador: Un Pueblo, Una Realidad* (Lima: CUAVES, 1984).

2. For an early examination of the Velasco urban policy and the invasion that led to the formation of Villa El Salvador, see David Collier, *Squatter and Oligarchs: Authoritarian Rule and Policy Change in Peru* (Baltimore: Johns Hopkins University Press, 1976), pp. 97–123.

3. For an exhaustive review of the physical evolution of Villa El Salvador, see Jorge Burga and Claire Delpech, *Villa El Salvador: La Ciudad y su Desarollo* (Lima: CIED, 1989).

4. Antonio Aragón, interview by author in Lima, May 22, 1989.

5. Antonio Aragón, "La CUAVES: Un Simbolo, Una Esperanza," in CELADEC, *Villa El Salvador: De Arenal a Distrito Municipal* (Lima: CELADEC, 1983), p. 26.

6. Antonio Aragón, interview with author in Lima, May 22, 1989.

7. Cited in Antonio Aragón, "La CUAVES: Un Simbolo, Una Esperanza," p. 20.

8. Since the founding of CUAVES, additional secretariats have been added, including those for women's affairs, human rights, and youth.

9. Fernando Tuesta, "Villa El Salvador: Izquierda, Gestión Municipal y Organización Popular," Unpublished manuscript, Lima: 1988, p. 7.

10. Odilón Mucha, "En los Arenales de Lurín," in CELADEC, *Villa El Salvador: De Arenal a Distrito Municipal*, p. 36.

11. DESCO, *Cronología Política: 1976* (Lima: DESCO, 1977), p. 2241.

12. Fernando Tuesta, "Villa El Salvador: Izquierda, Gestión Municipal y Organización Popular," p. 19.

13. In his study of the Peruvian church, Klaiber points out that Peru lacked "a 'rebel Church' in the popular sector. To a large degree this fact is due to the efforts of spokesmen and leaders of the 'popular' Church ... to strengthen their ties with the bishops." Jeffrey Klaiber, *La Iglesia en el Perú* (Lima: Pontificia Universidad Católica, 1988), p. 421.

14. Michel Azcueta, interview by author in Lima, May 24, 1989.

15. Villa El Salvador, "Acta de Compromiso Entre CUAVES-Municipio" (Lima: Municipalidad de Villa El Salvador, 1984).

16. CUAVES, "Acatamiento de las Listas de Candidatos al Concejo Distrital Frente a la CUAVES" (Lima: CUAVES, 1986).

17. Michel Azcueta, interview by author in Lima, May 24, 1989. Azcueta admitted that the budgetary process in Villa is informal and legally questionable, but suggested that popular participation should not be impeded by legal "technicalities."

18. Henry Pease García, *Democracia y Precariedad Bajo el Populismo Aprista* (Lima: DESCO, 1988), pp. 77–113.

19. Cited in Peri Paredes, "La Instrumentalización Política del PAIT," Unpublished manuscript, Lima: 1988, pp. 211–212.

20. Paredes, "La Instrumentalización Política del PAIT," pp. 204–207.

21. Interestingly, Villa's participation in the PAIT program was approved by the CUAVES in 1985. Clearly, few suspected the degree to which it would be used for clientelist purposes.

22. A comparative discussion on the emergence and impact of new social movements in Latin America is found in Arturo Escobar and Sonia Alvarez, eds., *The Making of Social Movements in Latin America: Identity, Strategy and Democracy* (Boulder: Westview Press, 1992); and David Slater, *New Social Movements and the State in Latin America* (Amsterdam: CEDLA, 1985). One of the most comprehensive theoretical analyses of the implications of social movements is found in Sidney Tarrow, *Power in Movement: Social Movements, Collective Action and Politics* (Cambridge: Cambridge University Press, 1994).

23. Centro de Estudios Cristianos y Capacitación Popular (CECYCAP), *Comedores Familiares: Manual de Organización, Roles y Funciones* (Arequipa: CECYCAP, n.d.).

24. The program was designed primarily by IU councilmen Oscar Ugarte and Henry Pease García.

25. On the development of the women's movement in Villa, see Cecilia Blondet, *Las Mujeres y el Poder: Una Historia de Villa El Salvador* (Lima: Instituto de Estudios Peruanos, 1991).

7

Sendero Luminoso:
Ideology and the State in the Andes

During the 1980s the figure of Presidente Gonzalo and his images of fanaticized masses and bloody revolution dominated Peru's politics. Gonzalo's organization, Sendero Luminoso (Shining Path), was the most important insurgent group to emerge in Peru in the last two centuries. Known for its brutal methods and rigid ideology, Sendero's successful expansion from a largely rural and isolated insurgency to a nationwide movement took both Peru and the world by surprise. Although the capture and incarceration of Gonzalo in 1992 significantly crippled Sendero's organization and strategy, its activities will have a lasting impact on state-society relations in Peru for decades. This chapter argues that Sendero's rapid growth in the 1980s and early 1990s was directly related to limits in the state's organizational capacities and influence in society.

The first part of this chapter will examine the Maoist fundamentalism of Sendero and its relation to state policies. The widespread political radicalization that resulted from state policies during the 1970s certainly laid the basis for a greater acceptance of Sendero's discourse that initially differed little from other radical leftists.[1] Among the radicalized parties and groups of that period, Sendero Luminoso staked out the most extreme position by carrying out anti-system opposition through violence, where others only preached violence. The group's organization also played an important part in its rapid expansion. Sendero Luminoso's organization followed the classic Maoist model used by many other groups in Peru, but it was far more successful in taking advantage of the state's weakest points.

The second part of this chapter focuses on how the organizational limits of the state contributed to the expansion of insurgency. Historically, state-society relations in the Andean highlands relied upon a series of

TABLE 7.1 Terrorist Attacks by Department and Region, 1980–1989

Department	1980	1981	1982	1983	1984	1985	1986	1987	1988	1989
Ancash	10	29	38	24	15	68	53	116	98	242
Apurímac	9	17	53	12	23	17	139	107	140	68
Ayacucho	48	150	323	460	655	362	354	404	390	381
Cajamarca	5	26	33	20	15	21	24	98	67	117
Cusco	8	75	29	32	30	68	69	47	35	30
Huancavelica	9	7	39	78	183	163	111	68	111	106
Huánuco	0	2	3	13	79	84	55	100	119	160
Junín	31	54	42	68	84	174	169	242	326	594
Pasco	4	16	19	42	89	131	113	132	101	139
Puno	3	24	12	25	59	63	277	63	52	103
Highlands	127	400	591	774	1232	1151	1364	1377	1439	1940
Arequipa	15	22	24	31	41	35	99	81	81	53
Ica	0	14	19	7	23	16	14	23	64	85
La Libertad	6	17	29	23	95	151	125	123	84	100
Lambayaque	12	15	25	15	21	68	66	42	75	52
Lima	38	190	178	256	292	589	834	696	513	642

117

Moquegua	1	14	2	0	1	18	0	11	0	1
Piura	1	4	0	4	27	7	16	25	25	39
Tacna	3	20	17	3	0	4	4	7	7	23
Tumbes	0	0	0	0	1	2	1	11	14	6
Coast	76	372	294	339	501	890	1159	1019	863	1001
Amazonas	0	6	2	2	1	0	2	0	1	4
Loreto	6	11	3	3	1	18	0	11	3	18
Madre de Dios	0	0	1	0	1	0	0	0	1	0
San Martín	0	0	0	4	11	8	23	65	83	77
Ucayali	10	2	0	1	13	1	0	26	27	107
Amazon Basin	16	18	6	10	27	27	24	102	115	206
Total	219	714	891	1123	1760	2068	2547	2498	2415	3147

Source: 1980–87, author's elaboration of Ministry of Interior figures from DESCO, *Violencia Política en el Perú* (Lima: DESCO, 1989), p. 28. 1988–89 figures from Richard Webb and Graciela Fernández Baca, *Perú en Numeros* (Lima: Cúanto SA, 1991), p. 335. The figures include all terrorist attacks, including those from MRTA, which started its activities in 1984.

TABLE 7.2 Principal Targets of Terrorist Attacks, 1980–1988

	May 1980– July 1985	*August 1985– June 1988*
Police Stations	412	454
Electric Towers	390	549
Banks	135	329
Bridges	69	96
Private Houses	–	411
Government Buildings[a]	125	210
Population Centers	–	213
Political Groups	104	202

[a] Includes Electoral Registers, CORDES, Special Projects and Municipalities.

Source: Senado de la República, *Violencia y Pacificación* (Lima: Senado de la República, 1989), vol. 3, appendix.

intermediary relations with local landed elites through whom the central government made its norms felt. When the military's reforms did away with local elite structures, a political vacuum developed. By the 1980s Sendero Luminoso was well-positioned to benefit from and expand that vacuum, meeting the social needs of many in the Andes more successfully than the state.

Unlike most previous violent movements in Peru, Sendero Luminoso is a revolutionary insurgency, an armed minority group dedicated to violently overthrowing the established political and economic order and replacing it with an alternative system of relationships. Rebels or rioters may attack and attempt to destroy the existing political or economic structures, but generally lack a coherent ideological alternative to replace the system. By contrast, insurgents promise to substitute the entire economic and political system with completely new structures. Rebels or other violent groups may develop into revolutionary insurgencies, but categorization should be determined by a group's tactics, strategy, and ideology, rather than their success or failure.[2] Revolutionary challengers like Sendero Luminoso are "contenders" for state power who question the legitimacy and prerogatives of the state in society.[3] Such movements can only advance if groups in society accept them as legitimate and viable alternatives to the existing state. The terrain of society thus becomes a battleground for loyalty between the state and state contenders.

Perhaps the most surprising aspect of Sendero Luminoso was its rapid expansion. From its first actions in the remote confines of the southern highlands, Sendero quickly spread its activity to virtually every region of Peru. Table 7.1 illustrates the regional distribution of insurgent activities. From 1980 through 1989, over half of all attacks occurred in the Peruvian highlands. Ayacucho remained the department with the highest number of attacks, although its share of the national total steadily declined. Overall, terrorist attacks in the highlands increased ten-fold during the 1980s. However, attacks increased thirteen-fold in coastal areas between 1980 and 1988. Within that region, the greatest expansion occurred in Lima. Sendero dramatically increased attacks in the capital after 1988, and by 1990 most Sendero activity was being carried out in metropolitan Lima. The departments of San Martín and Ucayali witnessed greater insurgent activity after 1986, as Sendero became active in the coca-rich Alto Huallaga Valley.[4]

From Chairman Mao to President Gonzalo

The Social Roots of Maoism in Peru

Maoism, and Sendero's fundamentalist interpretation of Maoism, differ sharply from classic Marxist revolutionary practice, especially as carried out in Latin America. Unlike other Marxist currents, Maoism places special emphasis on the peasant as a revolutionary actor and suggests that violence is needed not only to achieve power but to "purify" revolutionary consciousness. Violence inspires revolutionary fervor by making the struggle of naked class interests palpable.[5] Maoism emphasizes a search for a new identity in rural and national traditions and openly rejects the urban, modern, and "westernized" sector of society. Maoism offers the "alternative" of a peasant utopia. As Mesnier correctly points out, "the Maoist tendency is to find the sources of socialism ... in a peasantry relatively uninvolved with capitalist socioeconomic relations and with intellectuals ideologically uncorrupted by bourgeois ideas."[6]

Both in ideological and organizational terms, Maoism has had far greater success in Peru than in any other country of the Western Hemisphere. Since the initial development of a Maoist current in the country in the early 1960s, Maoism has been an important and, at times, dominant force in the Peruvian left.[7] It is important to view the emergence and growth of Sendero within that context. The position Maoism occupied in Peru is based on a series of social and historical conditions including: (1) a large *campesino* movement in the southern highlands during the early 1960s in which Maoist political groups played a major role, (2) the educational explosion among popular sectors in rural areas of the southern highlands that produced a new provincial intelligentsia in the 1960s and 1970s, and (3) the persistent ethnic and cultural divisions that character-ize Peru. These factors created an important political base for Maoist groups by incorporating a radical Maoist discourse within the political identity of a wide sector of the rural peasantry and intelligentsia. Thus, a radicalized base sympathetic to Maoist discourse and practice already existed by the time Sendero launched its armed activity.

The first step toward radicalization in the countryside occurred with the 1956–64 peasant rebellion that resulted from dramatic structural changes in the agricultural sector. Declining prices and land shortages significantly reduced peasant incomes. Between 1957 and 1964, as peasant incomes dropped, the number of agrarian strikes quadrupled. Julio Cotler noted that this movement was especially important because, for the first time in this century, peasants not only attempted to destroy existing relations but also emphasized their "cultural references" by directing their activity through the traditional peasant community.[8]

The Communist Party was one of the few organizations to express interest in organizing peasant protests, sending numerous advisors and lawyers to assist peasants in the countryside. Yet its decision to send mili-tants to the countryside proved fatal, convincing many militants of the need for a rural-based revolution modeled on China's, instead of the urban-based strategy of the pro-Soviet party.[9] At the IV Communist Party Conference in January 1964, the Maoist bloc acquired a majority of the delegates and proclaimed the "recovery" of the party.[10] However, during the next decade the most important problem confronting Peru's Maoists was not government repression but the movement's incessant political divisions.

For example, almost immediately after its founding, the new PCP-Bandera Roja began to splinter. One of the most important divisions occurred in February 1970 at the party's second plenary meeting. The meeting was carried out clandestinely in Huamanga, Ayacucho, and pre-sided over by Dr. Abimael Guzmán Reynoso, a professor at the Univer-sity of Huamanga and one of Bandera Roja's founders. Guzmán criticized the party's lack of preparation for armed struggle. He had developed a strong following in Huamanga and nearby Huanta as a result of his efforts to protest the closing of the university and new fees for secondary schools. Those struggles united *campesino* demands for free and accessible education with the demands of students and teachers, creating an intel-lectual-peasant alliance unprecedented in Peru.[11] By the time Guzmán criticized Bandera Roja in 1970, he had already developed his own politi-cal base that began what he later termed "the reconstruction" of the party.

The alliance Guzmán and his followers forged in Huamanga around education issues demonstrated the growing importance during the 1960s of the state educational system and intellectuals in the countryside. That system had dramatically increased the number of students as well as reduced illiteracy. The expansion of the educational system included the founding of a large number of provincial universities. Between 1960 and 1977, the university population expanded a dramatic 654 percent in Peru, mostly in newly founded provincial universities.[12] Intellectuals from Lima flocked to these new centers of learning that exercised a particular attraction for those interested in questions of Andean identity.

Maoism was the political model that most appealed to many intellectuals in the Andean region. They viewed Maoism as a more suitable model for revolutionary change because of its rural bias, the semi-feudal nature of the highland region (a hacienda system with modes of servitude, social hierarchy, and deference based on differences between whites and *mistis* with indians), and the vast cultural gap between the Andes and Lima. The new students from provincial and peasant backgrounds found in Maoism a model of change that spoke more to their realities than the urban-based analyses of the pro-Moscow Communist Party.[13] One popular study of semi-feudalism in Lucanas (Ayacucho) argued that the revolutionary struggle should be based

> on the peasant as the conscious and active component of the guerrilla army, able to combine reciprocally the guerrilla struggle with productive agrarian labor and ideological and political work. This way of struggle and of work has given positive results as in the case of Vietnam, in the struggle of liberation against Yankee imperialism. ....[14]

Throughout the 1960s and early 1970s, Maoism acquired a significant following in the southern highlands where Maoist groups actively organized at the secondary school and university levels. As the state education system expanded, so did the presence of Maoist political groups, such as Patria Roja and Sendero Luminoso, that focused most of their organizational efforts on the rural educational system.[15] By the early 1970s Patria Roja dominated the teachers union at a national level, while in the capital of Ayacucho, the smaller Maoist group known as Sendero Luminoso had become the city's leading political force through its influence in the local university and secondary schools.

During the Velasco regime, as was noted in Chapter Two, Maoism grew in importance and legitimacy among the popular sector. Unlike most other leftist groups, Sendero Luminoso largely restricted its organizational activities to Ayacucho. Although the group's discourse was vir-

tually the same as many other leftist groups, its political practices were quite different. Sendero had no national presence in the union, peasant, or shantytown movements. Sendero's influence in the byzantine world of Peru's leftist parties and in the broader political arena was, therefore, minimal. Throughout the decade, as other Maoist groups acquired an important national presence, Sendero remained isolated in Ayacucho, restricting its organization around the university where Abimael Guzmán taught. As a result, when Sendero decided to launch its insurgency in 1980, it was not viewed as an important political actor even in the small world of Maoist politics.

Organizing for an Alternative State

Although Sendero Luminoso never succeeded in creating what its leader termed a "strategic equilibrium," its organization was highly sophisticated, designed to carry out its war against the state while offering an alternative structure. For much of the 1980s, a cloud of secrecy surrounded Sendero's organizational structure. With its leaders in hiding, Sendero's propaganda created a mythical image of Abimael Guzmán, alias Presidente Gonzalo. Underlying this secrecy was the image Sendero projected of its ability to strike out at its enemies anywhere it chose, claiming that the "eyes and ears" of the party were everywhere. Attacks against retired military officials, among other party "enemies," led many to believe that at the very least Sendero had a highly developed intelligence network that could infiltrate even the security forces.[16]

A key factor in Sendero's ability to maintain secrecy was its cell-like structure. Members of a cell generally did not come into contact with other cells or with their superiors. The so-called "popular committees" were responsible for coordinating these cells.[17] These committees functioned in designated zones throughout the country and were responsible for the political activities of the party in their zones. Such activities included political education and propaganda, organizing the productive functions of their zones (including setting prices or regulating sales to markets), administering revolutionary justice, and guaranteeing security from military attacks or common crimes. The leading comisar of each committee was a secretary comisar who was also leader of the military wing of the party in his zone—the Ejército Guerrillero Popular (EGP). This linked the party apparatus with the military apparatus and assured the subordination of the latter. According to Gonzalo, these committees were the basis for creating a "new power" in the country. The term "new power" was used frequently in Sendero's literature to refer to its alternative state structures. Sendero described these structures as constituting the basis for a new state it termed the *República Popular de Nueva Democra-*

cia. Each element of its organization was seen as a building block for this alternative state:

> These *comités populares* have grown a hundred fold, those which are in an area form a support base, and a group of these the Popular Republic of New Democracy (RPND) in formation. In this way, there emerged the committees, the support bases and the newly emerging RPND.[18]

Support groups for Sendero were designed to act semi-clandestinely but, like the popular committees, they also acted as the bases for the RPND state. Largely created in metropolitan Lima, these organizations targeted urban groups, including union, neighborhood, and student organizations. One such group, Socorro Popular, provided aid to captured *Senderistas* in prison and their families. Through the Association of Democratic Attorneys it also provided legal counsel for members of Sendero about to be tried.[19] The most powerful of the support groups, however, was the Movimiento Obrero de Trabajadores Clasistas (MOTC), designed to win over workers in Lima's industrial belt along the Central Highway. The MOTC was critical in organizing the "armed strikes" carried out between 1989 and 1992 in Lima, that halted much of the city's normal business activity. Its members, who never numbered more than one hundred, organized factory takeovers, the burning of buses, the intimidation of union members affiliated with the CGTP, and the spread of graffiti in the area.[20]

The central committee was by far the most important organ of Sendero Luminoso and its members constituted an exclusive elite. They were the only ones to have direct access to Abimael Guzmán who, by all indications, presided over many of its meetings. Committee members were close associates of Guzmán and included a large number of women. Guzmán apparently set the agenda for strategy, though both he and the central committee responded to the needs and demands of regional commanders.

One of the most important organizational characteristics of Sendero was its success in fashioning groups at the local level to respond to local conditions. Sendero very effectively micromanaged local conflicts for its own purposes, putting those conflicts into the context of its overall structure. Abstract oppressors like the "bourgeoisie" were transformed into the local shopkeeper who overcharges, the corrupt mayor, and the abusive police.[21] Given the strong regional disparities in Peru, a policy of fighting thousands of "little wars" simultaneously was highly effective. It allowed Sendero to gain adherents by appearing as defenders of coca-growing peasants in the Huallaga Valley, landless peasants disputing cooperatives in Puno, and land invaders in the shantytowns of Lima. The ability of Sendero to integrate these conflicts into a national strategy aimed at challenging the state in society goes a long way in explaining the rapid expansion of its insurgency.

State Vacuum and the Social Base of Sendero

The Collapse of State-Society Intermediation

The historical abandonment of rural areas by the state was based on a pattern of development emphasizing control of the Andean highlands through a network of powerful local brokers.[22] During most of the Republican period of the nineteenth and early twentieth centuries, national politics was Lima politics. Centralization, a legacy of what was the most powerful viceroyalty of the Americas, determined that all local officials from prefect to governor be appointed by the Lima-based bureaucracy. A centralized state, however, is not synonymous with a powerful state. Although decisions emanated from Lima, and specifically from the presidential palace, the implementation of decisions beyond the limits of the "City of Kings" did not rely on a centralized bureaucracy, but on local brokers. This system lasted until the 1960s, breaking down only during the Chilean occupation of Lima in the 1880s.[23]

Power brokers, or *gamonales*, were prominent individuals, generally landowners, who maintained vast powers over the local population through a strong system of patron-client relations, or what Cotler termed a "triangle without base." Such a triangular relation implied that subordinates had clientelist ties with a patron at the top of an authority pyramid, but that clients rarely had horizontal ties among themselves. The *gamonal*, however, was not only a patron providing services in return for absolute obedience, but also an intermediary or broker between national institutions, such as the central government, and clients.[24] This system of intermediation proved useful to the *gamonal*, who acquired authority and legitimacy, and to the central government, which ensured that order could be enforced at low cost in regions of the country far from the capital and without a bureaucratic structure. The power of the *gamonal* over the local population was extensive and was enhanced by the ethnic divisions prevalent in Peru.

The end of this system of domination began in the 1950s as the power of local *gamonales* declined in the face of a serious agricultural crisis. This crisis not only led to growing peasant organization and revolt, but also accelerated the migratory trend toward the cities by both the peasantry and bankrupt elites. Nonetheless, it was not until the agrarian reform of the Velasco regime that the system came to a definitive end. In one fell swoop, the traditional landed oligarchy of the highlands was eliminated and the system of relations which had sustained them was destroyed.

The military regime hoped to replace patron-client relations with a corporatist system of representation in the countryside. The new agrarian cooperatives were designed to provide a crucial link between the state and society. Yet as we saw in Chapter Two, the military's corporatist project came to an end in the mid-1970s, defeated by a lack of resources, organization, and ultimately support by those whom it was supposed to represent. In its place there emerged the radical *clasismo* of militant parties and unions bent on weakening and overthrowing the state. In many areas of the country, cooperatives persisted but with managements that were often resented by neighboring peasants who did not benefit from the land reform. In areas such as Andahuaylas, Puno, and Junín, cooperative managers were viewed as a new oligarchy, monopolizing local politics, agrarian credits, and government attention.[25] The result of the military's reform project in the countryside, therefore, was to eliminate the existing mechanisms of intermediation and domination, without establishing new structures. With its sophisticated internal organization and fundamentalist ideology, Sendero was well-positioned to fill this gap in state-society relations.

The Social Base of Sendero

Sufficient evidence exists on the composition of Sendero's social base to arrive at conclusions regarding their support among Peru's popular sectors. Early studies by North American scholars suggested that Sendero's support base was the Ayacucho peasantry, driven into rebellion by a crisis of subsistence and an insensitive state bureaucracy.[26] These studies focused on the Ayacucho peasantry as the only substantial social base of Sendero. The rapid expansion of Sendero beyond Ayacucho and into other areas of the highlands, the Amazonian basin, and urban centers such as Lima, clearly indicated its social base was far wider than was initially suspected.

Most studies suggested that Sendero's support came from a wide cross-section of Peru's lower-classes. Its greatest support was found among three groups: the poor peasantry throughout the Andean highlands, provincial intellectuals including secondary and university students, and urban lower-class migrants with access to higher education. In all three groups, the greatest propensity to join Sendero occured among those under twenty-five years of age.

In an important study of condemned terrorists, 58 percent were found to come from the poorest areas of the country, all located in the highlands.[27] Confirming these results, studies done in Ayacucho, Andahuaylas, Junín, and Puno found that the greatest support for Sendero was among the poorest peasants, including those who were landless or working as journeymen.[28] In the case of urban areas, Sendero developed a strong base of support in shantytown districts where recent migrants from the Andean region had settled. In metropolitan Lima, Sendero was strongest in the newest and poorest settlements, such as Huaycán in the eastern sector of Lima. In older established popular sector neighborhoods, such as San Martín de Porras, Sendero's presence was limited.[29] However, the new shantytowns of Lima tended to lack the strong organizational networks, like those found in Villa El Salvador, that channeled social and economic protests through communal groups and/or leftist electoral parties.

Education was an important factor in all recent studies of Sendero's social base. Among those condemned for terrorism, the number with some university education was extremely high—35.5 percent. By contrast, among those condemned for other crimes, only 5.8 percent had a university education.[30] This level of university education among condemned terrorists was especially stunning if we consider that among the general population only 9 percent have some university education. University education among condemned terrorists was nearly four times higher than that of the general population.

The higher educational level found among Sendero militants also provided a strong indication of other important aspects of Sendero's social base. First, students and intellectuals have had a strong presence in Sendero Luminoso since the founding of the organization at the University of Huamanga. Most of the top and middle-level leadership were associated with a university or had strong ties with higher education.[31] The importance of this sector continued through the 1980s. Students alone represented 25 percent of those condemned for terrorism in Peru between 1983 and 1986.[32] Because the majority of those captured and convicted were from rural regions, one can conclude that the majority of students in this population were from provincial, rather than Lima-based universities. In a study by Chávez de Paz, sixty-five students in his sample were convicted terrorists. Thirty-two of them specified their university and twenty of these were from provincial universities. Moreover, the universities most mentioned in Lima were public universities with a high population of urban lower-class and migrant students.[33]

Youth was another important element in Sendero's social base. Chávez de Paz found that at least 60 percent of those convicted for terrorism were twenty-five or younger.[34] Sendero aggressively recruited in both high schools and universities, believing that it was easier to form a militant at an earlier age when students lacked prior political beliefs or experience. This explained Sendero's consistent practice of attempting to forcibly impose its teaching "methods" on rural schools and even kidnapping *campesino* children for ideological indoctrination.[35]

Sendero's ideological message presented these students with the possibility of a radical change in their social situations and, more importantly, a direct role in bringing about those changes. All of the groups that constituted Sendero's social base represented segments of society with a weak and precarious status in the social, economic, and political systems. As the country experienced dramatic structural changes after 1960, the groups that supported Sendero found their social and economic situation worsening. Reforms raised expectations that went largely unfulfilled for poor peasants, shantytown dwellers, and provincial intellectuals. The experience of Sendero Luminoso was, therefore, consistent with what is known regarding the type of groups and individuals likely to be attracted to revolutionary movements.[36]

A close examination of Sendero's discourse revealed how Maoism was interpreted and applied to Peru's daily realities.[37] For Sendero, Maoism represented the culmination of all history and the realization of a final "grand harmony" toward which "15 billion years of the history of material in motion ... moves necessarily and cannot be contained."[38] According to Sendero, history would move inextricably toward communism and the members of Sendero Luminoso would play a crucial role in this movement. Guzmán as President Gonzalo was considered the "fourth sword" of Communism, the fourth great contributor to Communist thought and practice after Marx, Lenin, and Mao. Maoism represented the third and final stage of Marxist thought which Guzmán applied to Peru, the launching point of world revolution.[39] In a world context where both Maoism and Communism declined as political forces, Sendero viewed itself as the only true source of revolution. Even as the Berlin Wall was falling, Sendero continued to view the world as dominated by North American imperialism, Soviet revisionism, and Deng Xiao Ping's "betrayal" of Mao in China.[40]

This doctrinal rigidity meant that Sendero was intent on a strict implementation of Maoist discourse and practice. The most basic element of this discourse was the heavily rural and "mass" orientation of strategy and rhetoric. Peasants were given a special role in this strategy:

> Armed struggle and the war of guerrillas is the path of surrounding the cities from the countryside. It is the application of Marxism-Leninism-Maoism, principally Maoism, to our reality. All that we have today is the work of the people and principally of the poor peasant, who with the correct direction of the PCP and its leader Presidente Gonzalo, today advances victoriously . ...[41]

Gonzalo himself reiterated the importance of the poor peasantry in Sendero's strategy in the following terms:

> Primarily the peasant participates, especially the poor peasant, as combatants and officials at all levels, in this way they participate. ... The 'new power' is only developed in the countryside, in the cities it will come at the final stage of the Revolution.[42]

Sendero used the acute ethnic and cultural differences that separated the largely indian, mestizo, urban and rural poor, from the white Lima-based elite in very specific ways. As with Mao's own discourse and practice, these ethnic differences were not mentioned overtly, but could only be seen through a careful review of revolutionary behavior. According to Sendero, the main protagonist and source of revolutionary identity was the peasantry, and primarily the poor Andean peasant, even though the actual social base of insurgency was far more inclusive. The peasant represented the new revolutionary man, freed from western and bourgeois values. In the Peruvian context, where traditional Andean culture with strong pre-Hispanic elements still existed among the peasantry, a close identification of peasant identity with revolutionary identity necessarily implied that Andean culture took on an important role in Sendero's conceptualization of class.

Sendero's newspaper, *El Diario*, openly addressed the relation between Andean culture and the revolution in several articles on Andean culture and "semi-feudalism" in the countryside. The close link established between revolutionary identity and Andean peasant culture was best illustrated in an article on the traditional songs of the region known as *huaynos*.

> Despite all the *huayno* advances—it belongs to the future—its culture advances, the *runa andino*, it advances from the Andes to Lima, from the countryside to the city, causing great joy among the proletariat and great nervousness among the bourgeoisie. The indian advances, the *cholo*, the *serrano* (there is a song that says 'Peru was born *serrano*'), *quechua* advances, as does *aymara, chanka, wanka*. ...[43]

The parallel established between these songs—the indian and *cholo*—and the revolution was clear: they advance from the countryside to the city, just as the Maoist revolution advances from the countryside to the city.

Sendero's insistence on the Maoist "cultural revolution" also indicated how culture and class were seen as inextricably linked. Mao insisted on cultural revolution as an effort to constantly purify revolutionaries and maintain their revolutionary identity. Following that path, Sendero argued that the purpose of a cultural revolution was far-reaching, eliminating not only the differences between classes but between the city and countryside, and between manual and intellectual labor. According to Sendero, only through a cultural revolution, or indeed successive cultural revolutions, could contradictions such as these be eliminated. What did cultural revolution imply for Sendero? Guzmán indicated that the peculiar situation of Peru meant that its cultural revolution must be based on Peru's own historical experience, though he failed to outline a specific agenda.[44]

Faced with the class and ethnic differences which divided Peruvian society, Sendero projected an alternative vision of Peru's society that was anti-urban and anti-western while reaffirming the indigenous, mestizo, peasant, and the poor. It was a vision of Peru as a rural utopia. Although this vision did not reflect the complex reality of Peruvian society, it did have a powerful appeal among the marginalized popular classes that remained estranged from the modern, white, urban society and state of Peru's elite.

Conclusion

This chapter examined the most important violent challenger for state power that Peru has confronted this century. The rapid growth of Sendero Luminoso during the 1980s demonstrated the difficulties confronting the state in society in the post-Velasco era. Although some of these difficulties, including deep ethnic and class divisions and a reliance on intermediaries to manage state-society relations were historically based, many were also the direct result of state policies. Land reform and educational policies dramatically changed rural structures and relations, creating new demands and pressures in the countryside that were unforeseen by policy makers. Paradoxically, while state policies helped change rural society, they were not very effective in shaping the type of social relations that resulted.

A key aspect of the explanation for Sendero's expansion focuses on the relation between Sendero and society. Sendero's strength was in its ability to understand and insert itself into local societal structures and conflicts and make its ideology relevant to the lives of many throughout the country. This task was aided by the absence of state institutions and authority in much of the countryside and by nearly two decades of Maoist discourse and practice in the Peruvian countryside. Its goal was to channel the frustrations and rage of marginal groups into a formidable organization directed not only at making war on the state but also at preparing to replace that state.

During most of the 1980s and early 1990s, Sendero's advance seemed almost inevitable. Some observers suggested the possibility of an ultimate Sendero victory or a devastating civil war. Indeed, up until the capture of Abimael Guzmán in September 1992, Sendero had suffered few serious setbacks. Guzmán's capture raised the question of why state actions against Sendero had been so ineffective for over a decade. The next chapter will explain the state's response to Sendero.

Notes

1. Many political documents from New Left parties of the 1970s read like Sendero documents of the 1980s. One document from Vanguardia Revolucionaria suggested, "The destruction of reactionary power means developing a prolonged and popular war. Revolutionary violence is the way to destroy this power; violence which will have as its focus the revolutionary activity of millions of workers and peasants." Vanguardia Revolucionaria, "Programa General de Vanguardia Revolucionaria" (Lima: VR, 1976), p. 73.

2. John Walton, *Reluctant Rebels* (New York: Columbia University Press, 1982), p. 11.

3. For a discussion of "contenders" see Charles Tilly, *From Mobilization to Revolution* (New York: Random House, 1978), pp. 98–142.

4. San Martín was also an important base for the Movimiento Revolucionario Tupac Amaru (MRTA), a small pro-Cuban guerrilla group active during the 1980s. The MRTA never acquired a significant social base and was largely eliminated after the capture of its top leaders in 1990 and 1991.

5. Among the best analyses of Maoist political theory are John Bryant Starr, *Continuing the Revolution: The Political Thought of Mao Tse-Tung* (Princeton: Princeton University Press, 1979); Edward Rice, *Mao's Way* (Berkeley: University of California Press, 1972); Chalmers Johnson, *Ideology and Politics in Contemporary China* (Seattle: University of Washington Press, 1972).

6. Mesnier refers to this as Mao's "populist-organic" conception of revolution. Maurice Mesnier, "Utopian Socialist Themes in Maoism," in John W. Lewis, ed., *Peasant Rebellion and Communist Revolution in Asia* (Stanford: Stanford University Press, 1974), p. 238. On Mao's theory of the peasantry, see Mao Tse-Tung, "Investigation of the Peasant Movement in Hunan," in Mao Tse-Tung, *The Collected Works of Mao Tse-Tung* (Beijing: Foreign Languange Press, n.d.), vol. 1, p. 345.

7. See Chapter Two.

8. Julio Cotler, *Clases, Estado y Nación* (Lima: Instituto de Estudios Peruanos, 1978), p. 289.

9. For a fascinating document about these events written in almost autobiographical prose, see Saturnino Paredes, *Acerca de la Historia del Partido y Sus Luchas Internas* (Lima: Ediciones Bandera Roja, 1968).

10. A version of events from the perspective of the pro-Soviet party (PCP-Unidad) is found in Jorge Del Prado, *Cuatro Facetas de la Historia del PCP* (Lima: Ediciones Unidad, 1987), p. 283.

11. Carlos Iván Degregori, *El Surgimiento de Sendero Luminoso: Ayacucho, 1969–1979* (Lima: Instituto de Estudios Peruanos, 1990).

12. Ibid., p. 46.

13. A series of fascinating interviews with such students is found in Nicolás Lynch, *Los Jóvenes Rojos de San Marcos: El Radicalismo Universitario de los Años Setenta* (Lima: El Zorro de Abajo, 1990).

14. Felix Valencia Quintanilla, *Luchas Campesinas en el Contexto Semi-Feudal del Oriente de Lucanas, Ayacucho* (Lima: CPEA, 1984), pp. 137–139.

15. PCP:Patria Roja Secretary General Alberto Morena, interview by author in Lima, August 15, 1988. The extensive network of teachers that exists "in every village of Peru" was an important reason behind their organization by the Maoist Patria Roja, according to its secretary general. He argued that the distribution of teachers provided an important base on which to build a national political organization.

16. For two cases involving high level infiltration, one involving the air force and the other a congressional commission, see *Caretas*, June 5, 1989, p. 21; and *Caretas*, August 5, 1991, p. 34.

17. Much of what is known of the structure of Sendero comes from its own documents. The most detailed discussion is found in a document released in May 1989 entitled, "Sobre El Comité Popular y sus Funciones," which describes the role of these committees and their relation to other Sendero organizations.

18. *El Diario*, July 24, 1988, p. 17.

19. Gabriela Tarazona-Sevillano, *Sendero Luminoso and the Threat of Narco-Terrorism* (New York: Praeger Publishers, 1991), pp. 64–65.

20. On Sendero's urban organization during this period, see *Sí*, June 12, 1989, p. 31; and *Caretas*, September 25, 1989, p. 32. Sendero's organization among industrial workers in Lima relied upon "infiltrating" existing unions as well as creating separate organizations.

21. Michael Smith, "Taking the High Ground: Shining Path and the Andes," in David Scott Palmer, ed., *The Shining Path of Peru* (New York: St. Martins Press, 1992), pp. 19–20.

22. See Chapter One.

23. For the effects of the War of the Pacific on state-society relations in the highlands, see Nelson Manrique, *Yawar Mayu: Sociedad Terrateniente en la Sierra, 1879–1900* (Lima: DESCO, 1987).

24. Julio Cotler, "Internal Domination and Social Change in Peru," in Irving Louis Horowitz, ed., *Masses in Latin America* (New York: Oxford University Press, 1970), pp. 407–444.

25. See Ronald Berg, "Sendero Luminoso and the Peasantry of Andahuaylas," *Journal of Inter-American Studies and World Affairs* 28:4, Winter 1986–1987, pp. 164–197.

26. One of the first studies to suggest this was Cynthia McClintock's "Why Peasants Rebel: The Case of Peru's Sendero Luminoso," *World Politics* 27:1, pp. 48–84; and David Scott Palmer, "Rebellion in Rural Peru: The Origins and Evolution of Sendero Luminoso," *Comparative Politics* 18:2, pp. 127–146. For a sharp critique of the approach U.S. scholars have taken toward Sendero, see Deborah Poole and Gerardo Renique, "The New Chroniclers of Peru: US Scholars

and Their 'Shining Path' of Peasant Rebellion," *Bulletin of Latin American Research* 10:2, 1986, pp. 133–191.

27. Dennis Chávez de Paz, *Juventud y Terrorismo* (Lima: Instituto de Estudios Peruanos, 1989), p. 34.

28. See Henri Favre, "Peru: Sendero Luminoso y Horizontes Oscuros," *QueHacer* 31, October 1984, pp. 25–35; José Luis Renique, "Estado, Partidos y Lucha por la Tierra en Puno," *Debate Agrario* 1, 1987, pp. 55–76; Nelson Manrique, "Politica y Violencia en el Perú," *Margenes* 5, March 1990, pp. 137–182.

29. On Huaycán see especially *Caretas*, June 26, 1989, p. 31.

30. Chávez de Paz, *Juventud y Terrorismo*, p. 42.

31. *Caretas*, January 29, 1990, pp. 39–41; *La República*, January 28, 1990, p. 7. The case of Juan Carlos "Gringo" Olivares, a political-military commander of Sendero in the Puno region, is a good example. Olivares was the son of an Aprista intellectual in Arequipa and attended the Jesuit-run San José and the Universidad Santa María before turning to Maoism.

32. Ibid., p. 49.

33. Ibid., p. 49. The schools are: UNM San Marcos, Universidad Nacional de Ingeniería, Universidad Nacional de Tacna and Universidad Nacional Agraria.

34. Chávez de Paz, *Juventud y Terrorismo*, p. 29.

35. Manuel Granados, "El PCP-SL: Aproximación a su Ideología," *Socialismo y Participación* 37, March 1987.

36. The literature on the type of social actors or personalities most attracted to violent movements is quite extensive. See Michael Walzer, *The Revolution of the Saints: A Study in the Origins of Radical Politics* (Cambridge: Harvard University Press, 1965); Samuel Huntington, *Political Order in Changing Societies* (New Haven: Yale University Press, 1968); Tedd Robert Gurr, *Why Men Rebel* (Princeton: Princeton University Press, 1970); Walter Reich, *Origins of Terrorism: Psychologies, Ideologies, States of Mind* (Cambridge: Cambridge University Press, 1990).

37. The following analysis was based on a careful review of *El Diario*, Sendero's daily newspaper during 1987–1989, as well as a thorough reading of all major Sendero documents publicly released between 1981 and 1989. One of the first documents made public was "Desarollemos la Guerra de Guerrillas," (Lima: PCP-SL, 1982).

38. PCP-SL, "Desarollar la Guerra Popular Sirviendo a la Revolución," (Lima: PCP-SL, 1986), p. 20.

39. *El Diario*, July 24, 1988, pp. 4–5.

40. The advent of *perestroika* in the former USSR appeared to reaffirm Sendero's belief that only it represented the true path to communism. Sendero argued that *perestroika* would inevitably lead to the ills associated with capitalism, going so far as to link AIDS with capitalism. *El Diario*, March 15, 1990, p. 13.

41. *El Diario*, May 17, 1988, p. 13.

42. *El Diario*, July 24, 1988, p. 11.

43. *El Diario*, May 8, 1988, p. 6; also *El Diario*, April 1988, p. 9. Sendero's newspaper also ran a series of articles condemning what it termed "folklore," or the commercial use of Andean culture, including concerts and records. See *El Diario*, June 28, 1989, p. 3.

44. *El Diario*, July 24, 1988, p. 36; and *El Diario*, July 1988, p. 10. Also see Partido Comunista del Perú, "Documentos Fundamentales del Primer Congreso del Partido Comunista del Perú," (Lima: PCP-SL, 1988).

8

State Capacities
and Counterinsurgency

The cohesiveness of the state apparatus and its ability to mobilize society have been key elements in limiting the expansion of insurgent challenges. State strategies in countries such as Colombia, Venezuela, and El Salvador, where insurgent challenges were defeated or forestalled through negotiations were facilitated by relatively high degrees of elite consensus and state cohesion. In these countries, the state strengthened its claims to legitimacy and mobilized key sectors of society against insurgents through elections, dialogue with opposition groups, civic action programs, or social reforms.[1] In each of these cases, insurgents were incorporated into the existing political system either through military defeat (Venezuela) or a peace process (El Salvador, Colombia-M19).

The experience of Peru in the 1980s differs dramatically from the above cases. Peru's state had a limited capacity to mobilize society against Sendero Luminoso, especially in the highlands where the state's organizational capabilities and influence in society were weakest. The state's own policies from the 1960s onward and the deep social divisions that plagued the country, were significant factors inhibiting the development of strong state-society links against insurgency in the highlands. The lack of such links was aggravated by conflicts within the state over the nature of insurgency and the methods to combat it. Significant strides in overcoming these obstacles were made only in the early 1990s as part of Fujimori's attempt to restructure the state.

This chapter will evaluate state responses to insurgency during the 1980s and the changes in state counterinsurgency initiated by the Fujimori regime. First, state responses to Sendero between 1980 and 1989 will be examined. State elites were initially divided over how to respond to Sendero and unwilling to commit significant resources to the conflict.

These divisions reflected deep conflicts among differing state elites over the role of the state in society and even the nature of Peruvian society itself. Often following contradictory and conflicting methods and goals, state elites proved unable to effectively confront Sendero and, thus, contributed to its rapid expansion. Second, the changes implemented by the Fujimori regime between 1990 and 1995 will be analyzed. In the effort to "retool" the state, the security apparatus received special attention from the regime. This organizational restructuring was combined with new attempts on the part of the state to influence society in the highlands. Both efforts yielded important advances in counterinsurgency in a relatively short time.

The Military and Counterinsurgency, 1980–1989

Within a year of the transition to civilian rule, security forces became involved in national politics. The transition promised a reduced role for the military in politics. Yet the emergence of Sendero quickly drew the military directly into political conflicts once again. Sendero Luminoso carried out its first armed action in 1980 during the first presidential elections in seventeen years. The increased political role the armed forces acquired over the following years resulted more from civilian pressures than the military's own appetite for a return to power. At the end of military rule, the Peruvian armed forces were demoralized, divided, and intent on restoring their shattered unity by depoliticizing the institution. However, civilian officials openly encouraged the military to increase its role in counterinsurgency planning and operations.

The state was initially slow to respond to the challenge of Sendero Luminoso. During the first two years of guerrilla activity, government officials wrongly characterized Sendero as either being composed of "common delinquents" seeking personal profit and publicity, or agents of a foreign communist power. Various political parties interpreted Sendero's activities as representing the covert actions of their opponents.[2] In retrospect, all of these characterizations betrayed a stunning ignorance of the situation in the Andean highlands by Lima-based elites. Belaúnde's government initially responded to insurgency by deploying more police in affected areas. The Peruvian police, divided into separate forces (Guardia Republicana and Guardia Civil) with different command structures and responsibilities, were plagued by internal bickering, a lack of training, and few resources to fight a full scale insurgency. Moreover, throughout the Andean highlands the police were distrusted by the local population because of their reputation for corruption and abuse of power. These problems impeded any possibility of a successful counterinsurgency campaign. By the end of 1982 it became apparent that a significant change of strategy was needed. Sendero had expanded beyond its original base in Ayacucho and was carrying out actions throughout the highlands as well as in Lima.

Recognizing the increased threat that Sendero's activities represented, President Belaúnde invoked his authority under the 1979 Constitution to declare states of emergency in seven provinces of the south-central highlands. During these states of emergency, security forces were given extraordinary powers while individual liberties, including *habeaus corpus*, were suspended.[3] Belaúnde also created military commands in emergency zones, known as *Comandos Politicos-Militares*, granting the armed forces complete political authority. For all practical purposes, the commanders of these zones became military governors, responsible only to the military hierarchy and not to local elected officials, congress, or the judiciary. Although the emergency zones were initially restricted to the highlands, they were quickly created wherever insurgent activity took place. By 1990 approximately sixty provinces throughout the country, including Lima, had been declared emergency zones.

As a result of President Belaúnde's decision, the military took charge of Peru's counterinsurgency strategy. In 1983 responsibility for counterinsurgency strategy was turned over to the joint command of the armed forces (Comando Conjunto). In reality, strategy and tactics depended on the commander (Jefe Político-Militar) in a particular emergency zone. Moreover, relying on the military command for strategy with almost no civilian oversight tended to produce conflicting tactics, depending on the vision of particular commanders. This situation increased the possibilities for internal divisions and conflicts in the armed forces. The lack of direct civilian control or formal oversight mechanisms also produced massive human rights violations.

The first military commander in Ayacucho was General Clemente Noel Moral, a former director of the National Intelligence Service (SIN) under the military government. Noel viewed Sendero Luminoso as part of a worldwide communist conspiracy and his approach to counterinsurgency, shared by Minister of Interior General Luis Cisneros, was similar to that followed during the 1970s by military regimes in the Southern Cone.[4] Subversives were broadly defined as all ideological opponents. Under this "national security doctrine" elaborated by the militaries of Argentina, Uruguay, and Brazil, subversives were not only defined as armed combatants, but also as those in the media, universities, and other social institutions who questioned the established order. As such, they were all considered legitimate targets of military actions.

The result in Peru, as in the Southern Cone, was a massive violation of human rights that included torture, extrajudicial executions, and forced disappearances.[5] These methods brought increased scrutiny of the military by regime opponents and the media. The most publicized case of violations occurred in Uchuraccay when peasant civil defense patrols organized by the army assassinated eight journalists. The case galvanized opponents to the military's growing authority and ultimately led to the removal of Noel. Criticism of the armed forces was intense and, clearly, military officers were unaccustomed to being held responsible for their actions. The military's new political responsibilities made it a legitimate target of open political criticism. In response to such criticisms, the armed forces grew increasingly defensive, accusing critics of being "traitors" interested in denigrating the institution.[6]

One of the most important problems the military confronted between 1983 and 1986 was a lack of consensus over the basic approach to counterinsurgency. Disillusioned by the hard-line tactics of General Noel, the military command turned to a "developmentalist" strategy. The new strategy had deep roots in the thinking of some Peruvian officers, and argued for dealing with insurgency by addressing the socioeconomic causes that lead people to support insurgents.[7] In early 1984 the new commander of the Ayacucho emergency zone declared that the only way to combat Sendero Luminoso was by combatting "poverty and rural neglect."[8] General Adrián Huamán, a fluent speaker of *quechua* from the highlands, argued for military involvement in a variety of social and economic development projects.[9]

The promise of Huamán's new strategy was quickly dashed by the conflict it created both within the military and between the military and the Belaúnde administration. While many within the military felt uncomfortable assuming greater governing authority throughout the country, the Belaúnde administration grew increasingly wary of Huamán's public statements that were eerily reminiscent of the Velasco regime. When those statements became critical of the civilian regime, Belaúnde and the military's high command agreed to remove Huamán from his sensitive post in Ayacucho. Although this ended the immediate crisis, the military as an institution remained divided over its role in counterinsurgency and its new political responsibilities.[10]

The election of Alan García in 1985 held the promise of a new beginning for counterinsurgency efforts. García campaigned on a platform of new initiatives in counterinsurgency, including peace negotiations, greater efforts to subordinate the military to civilian control, and increased respect for human rights. In addition, he promised to intensify the "developmentalist" efforts of Huamán, but with the civilian bureaucracy rather than the military in charge of civil aid programs and projects. Yet despite these promises, the García administration quickly found itself confronting the same structural limits on state capacities as its predecessor.

The first such limitation continued to be conflicts over strategy within the armed forces and between the armed forces and civilians. Despite a renewed emphasis on human rights and developmentalism, massacres and other violations continued. Shortly after García took office, a massacre of peasants occurred near Ayacucho. García vowed that those responsible would be held accountable and he dismissed several high-ranking officials, causing a major confrontation with the military's high command.[11] Yet a year later, the pattern of civilian abuses and military impunity reasserted itself. In June 1986 some 300 Sendero prisoners were killed during a prison riot, most executed by military forces after surrendering.[12] Only one lower-ranking officer was ever prosecuted, even though the massacre apparently occurred with the knowledge of several senior officers.

Although human rights violations declined during the first two years of García's administration, the type and pattern of violations did not change dramatically (see Table 8.1). By 1987 the regime had apparently deferred to resurgent hard-liners within the military on the issue. Human rights abuses rebounded and in several cases, particularly the 1988 Cayara massacre, local military commanders defied congressional investigators and civilian prosecutors. Despite García's early efforts to assert civilian control over counterinsurgency strategy, decision making remained largely in the hands of the military.

A counterinsurgency strategy based upon "developmentalism" remained popular throughout the mid-1980s, but military officials found it increasingly difficult to sustain.[13] The rapid expansion of Sendero's activities pressured security forces and the administration to find solutions that could offer immediate results. Moreover, the cut-off of foreign funding as a result of Peru's stand on the debt issue, effectively eliminated the possibility of using outside assistance to finance development projects in depressed highland areas. Nor could the Peruvian state supply the resources needed to improve the economy of the southern highlands. Most development projects started in the mid-1980s were abandoned and no new significant programs were undertaken. Peru's economic crisis also affected basic military preparedness. Salaries and operational capabilities declined drastically during the late 1980s, while corruption increased. Most of the country's military helicopters were grounded due to a lack of fuel or spare parts.[14] The discontent that resulted, especially among the officer corps, led to a rise in resignations as well as desertions.[15] Corruption also began to take its toll on the military. As the armed forces were increasingly deployed in areas where drug trafficking was rampant, the temptation to benefit from this lucrative trade affected personnel of all ranks.[16]

TABLE 8.1   Casualties of Political Violence and Disappearances, 1980–1990

	1980	1981	1983	1984	1985	1986	1987	1989	1988	1989	1990
Police	–	6	31	52	56	45	100	139	137	229	163
Military	–	–	1	9	26	31	29	53	143	109	135
Terrorists[a]	9	71	109	1,226	1,721	630	781	341	404	1,175	1,879
Civilians	2	5	41	655	1,750	712	416	362	734	1,365	1,531
Others[b]	–	–	11	27	35	19	50	41	91	–	–
Total	11	82	193	1979	3,588	1,437	1,376	1,136	1,508	2,878	3,708
Disappeared	–	–	–	696	574	253	214	69	293	308	302

[a] Alleged members of subversive groups.
[b] Includes political authorities, clergy and foreigners.

Source: DESCO (Lima), Data Bank on Political Violence; information on the Disappeared provided by Commission on Human Rights (Lima).

In addition to economic constraints and conflicts involving the military, the state's organizational effort was also hampered by rigid institutional rules. For example, military commanders in emergency zones were rotated on a yearly basis, preventing the accumulation of needed experience in counterinsurgency. Although these rules were initiated to prevent military officers from developing personal power bases, they also tended to produce a confusing change of strategies every year. Service rivalries also hampered security operations during most of the decade. The police and the military rarely coordinated their activities and this had deadly consequences. When police outposts were attacked by Sendero, the armed forces rarely came to their assistance. Rivalries between the army and navy resulted in the latter being assigned certain emergency zones in Ayacucho and the Huallaga Valley, largely for political rather than military reasons. Since the navy tended to be more hard-line in its approach to counterinsurgency than the army, adjacent zones were often governed with different policies.

By the end of the 1980s state efforts to counter the advance of Sendero were clearly not working and the prospect for enhancing state capabilities appeared minimal. Sendero's attacks became bolder, targeting elected officials and popular sector figures as well as the military. In the seventeen months leading up to the 1989 municipal elections, eighty-one mayors and councilmen had been assasinated by Sendero.[17] Frustration with the state's inability to counteract Sendero led to growing pressures for private, non-state responses. A paramilitary organization known as the Comando Rodrigo Franco (CRF) began attacking people it described as Sendero sympathizers.[18] The CRF labeled all ideological dissenters as subversives and targeted members of the legal left as well as suspected *Senderistas*. Paramilitary death squads and civil defense groups elsewhere in Latin America have generally had some connection with security forces.[19] Strong evidence existed that a similar situation had been reached in Peru. When García's prime minister suggested that the governing party should protect itself from terrorist attacks, many interpreted this as a signal for party militants to form paramilitary squads.[20] The privatization of violence that results when paramilitary groups become active, represents the ultimate abdication of state authority insofar as it cedes the monopoly on the legitimate use of force.

Restructuring State-Society Linkages, 1990–1995

The rapid expansion of Sendero Luminoso, which had gone almost unchecked during the Belaúnde and García periods, was halted during the first term of President Alberto Fujimori. After a decade of repeated failures in counterinsurgency, efforts were undertaken to address crucial weaknesses in the state's capabilities. The organizational reforms discussed in Chapter Five provided the state with new resources and improvements in the structure and coordination of security forces. The declines in military salaries and readiness were reversed, while a greater centralization of decision making took place. The impact of these reforms was felt almost immediately, as the state made its first gains against Sendero Luminoso in over a decade.

Many of those gains resulted from the greater emphasis given to intelligence agencies in counterinsurgency. The effective use of both police intelligence and the SIN were responsible for most of the major captures of *Senderistas* made during 1991 and 1992, including the capture of Abimael Guzmán. Intelligence agencies had played a minor role in counterinsurgency during the 1980s, even though most military theory and training on counterinsurgency suggested that they were a critical part of a successful strategy. The new emphasis on intelligence gathering and penetration was unfortunately not accompanied by a greater respect for human rights. Abuses committed by the armed forces continued and remained unpunished, and some evidence suggested that such abuses may have been sanctioned or planned by intelligence agencies as well as other anti-subversive special units.[21]

The centralization of decision making that occurred under the Fujimori regime created a strong tendency toward authoritarian practices. This was especially true regarding national security, where the regime seemed intent on providing the military with nearly absolute autonomy from legislative or judicial oversight in its counterinsurgency campaigns. Building on the impunity the military enjoyed during most of the Belaúnde and García periods, Fujimori attempted to codify the military's autonomy into law. Among the 120 decree laws Fujimori introduced in 1991, DL 171–90 stated that all military personnel in emergency zones must be tried in military courts, regardless of their crimes or the circumstances of their actions. Since these courts almost never condemned personnel for human rights abuses, the measure essentially provided immunity from prosecution.[22] The tendency to exonerate the actions of military officials reached a climax in June 1995 when Fujimori introduced a general amnesty for all military personnel.

One of the most intractable problems that plagued the counterinsurgency efforts of the 1980s was the persistent conflicts over counterinsurgency strategy and tactics within the armed forces, and between military officials and the civilian government. The Fujimori administration introduced the most dramatic reforms of the armed forces since the transition to civilian rule. The purpose of these reforms was to centralize decision making and increase the power of the president over the military. By early 1992 the command of the armed forces was in the hands of Fujimori's closest allies. Although the centralization turned the military into a virtual political ally of the regime's move towards authoritarianism, it also diminished the conflicts that hindered greater coordination in counterinsurgency during the 1980s.

Reforms enacted by presidential decree in 1991 increased the decision-making powers of the Joint Command of the Armed Forces, the National Defense Council, and the National Intelligence Service (SIN) regarding counterinsurgency strategy, and eliminated the role of the ministerial cabinet.[23] In addition, the heads of all the service branches were made to serve at the discretion of the president. As political appointees they could even serve beyond the legal retirement age. These changes reversed an important aspect of the "professionalization" of the armed forces started during the 1960s, with rules linking promotions to seniority, experience, and education, that were designed to prevent the emergence of *caudillos* within the military. With these rules overturned in 1991, the open identification of military officials with the civilian president became more prominent. Moreover, the Fujimori reforms gave broad new powers to military commanders in emergency zones while making them more directly responsible to the Joint Command. These changes effectively put counterinsurgency strategy into the hands of the president and his designated military chiefs and ended the multiple sources of authority, both civilian and military, that had produced many of the intra-military conflicts of the previous decade.

The most important aspect of the Fujimori regime's counterinsurgency strategy, however, was the civil defense patrols known as *rondas*. The *rondas* addressed one of the most important weaknesses that faced the state in its confrontation with Sendero Luminoso: its historically low presence and influence in much of highland society. Sendero's advance during the 1980s was largely possible through its ability to organize and address the needs of important sectors of highland society that had been neglected by the state. Without effective state influence, Sendero's strategy had concentrated on filling what it described as "political vacuums" in the region. The *rondas* were a clear attempt to contest and fill the gap through state-supported organizations, thus creating new intermediaries between the state and society.

The *rondas* predate the armed conflict with Sendero Luminoso. Originally created in the northern department of Cajamarca in the late 1970s, the *rondas* emerged to help peasants defend themselves against cattle rustlers, robbers, and corrupt local officials.[24] To many observers, the *rondas* represented local democracy and self-management, both of which have a long history in Peru. Over the years, they received organizational and

technical support from the Catholic Church, leftist parties, and NGOs.[25] At the start of the insurgent war, the armed forces developed civil defense patrols, also known as *rondas*, in Ayacucho. Unlike their counterparts in Cajamarca, these peasant *rondas* were organized, trained, and armed by the military to patrol remote areas and detain Sendero activity. The massacre of journalists in Uchurracay in 1983 by members of a *ronda* and the public outcry that followed sharply reduced the use of *rondas* in counterinsurgency. Uchurracay pointed out one of the key problems with a *ronda*-based strategy. Without strict control of their activities, *rondas* could develop into virtual private armies. Rather than strengthening state capabilities, they could help undermine them. The wariness regarding *rondas* existed even within the military which feared the possibility of arms being captured or *ronda* members joining Sendero.

Although *rondas* were not a central aspect of counterinsurgency between 1984 and 1986, they continued to exist particularly in areas of Ayacucho under the command of the navy. By the late 1980s, the García administration began to argue the need for *rondas*. The new turn toward *rondas* resulted from the apparent lack of viable alternative strategies. At the same time, growing sentiment in the ruling APRA party favored paramilitary or "private solutions" to insurgency. In a clear embrace of the *rondas*, President García traveled throughout the country in 1989 overseeing the arming of local *rondas*. The attitude of the military toward *rondas* had also apparently shifted. As the number of military patrols in the highlands was gradually reduced, *rondas* were seen as providing a frontline defense against Sendero's marauding armies. Nonetheless, problems persisted with their organization. Many *ronda* leaders in the Apurímac Valley of Ayacucho were involved in the lucrative drug trade of the area, while others used their new positions of authority to take over the land of nearby peasant communities.[26]

The new attention given to *rondas* in the last year of the García presidency was dramatically accelerated by the Fujimori regime. By the end of 1991, *rondas* were being formed throughout the country, from the center of drug trafficking in the Huallaga Valley to the shantytowns of Lima. In the central Andean department of Junín, *rondas* were created and armed by the local commander, General Luis Pérez Documet, at an unprecedented rate. The effects on insurgent activity were soon clear. Within three years terrorist attacks had been reduced in the area by nearly two-thirds.[27] The same levels of success occurred elsewhere, although often at a high cost. Members of *rondas* were special targets of Sendero, which ruthlessly attacked villages participating in military organized *rondas*.

During the Fujimori period *rondas* successfully competed with Sendero to fill the organizational gap that existed in state-society relations in much of the countryside. *Rondas* increasingly took on an intermediary role between the state and society, providing the type of linkages that had collapsed along with the agrarian reform. This role varied depending on the exact relation with the military in particular areas of the country. The *rondas* offered access to state resources (i.e. arms) to provide for their self-defense and usually food assistance or even some development aid. In return, the state acquired a capacity to mobilize and influence highland society that had eluded it during the previous decade of war. This mobilizing capacity, that has been crucial to all states in the region combatting insurgent challenges, ultimately proved the most successful element in the Fujimori effort to defeat Sendero. Nonetheless, it is too early to draw any conclusions about the long-term impact of *rondas* on state-society relations in the highlands after the dramatic decline of insurgency. The *rondas* may become the basis for a new penetration of Andean society by the state, or they may prove to have been yet another momentary intrusion into society by a distant state.

Conclusion

The Peruvian military's efforts to confront the insurgent challenge of Sendero Luminoso during the 1980s occurred in a context of conflicts within the armed forces over the nature of Sendero and how best to combat it. Added to these conflicts were institutional rigidities and an economic crisis that seriously affected the military's effectiveness. The difficulties the state had confronting Sendero were rooted in the dramatic decline in state capabilities since the mid-1970s. By the end of the decade, the state appeared to have run out of resources as well as ideas on how to counter the rapid expansion of Sendero.

The restructuring of the state's counterinsurgency efforts under the Fujimori regime illustrated the quick "retooling" of state capabilities. Improvements in military and intelligence capabilities were accompanied by a centralization of decision making. A renewed emphasis on the role of the *rondas* in counterinsurgency created new state-society relations in the highlands that could contest the growing social influence of Sendero Luminoso. These efforts yielded the most significant progress achieved against Sendero since the start of insurgency.

Throughout Peru's war with Sendero Luminoso a constant pattern of human rights abuses occurred. The ability of security forces to engage in such abuses or terrorize a population should not be confused with state capabilities. States with few capabilities are often, nonetheless, good at deploying brute force to intimidate opponents or challengers. The state's inherent monopoly of arms and legitimate use of force gives it significant

advantages in this area over social actors. Peru in the 1980s offered a good example of this distinction. An ineffective and weak state apparatus was still capable of violating basic human rights.

Both the insurgency of Sendero Luminoso and the difficulties the state encountered in combatting it, highlighted the limits of state capabilities in Peru. These difficulties were encountered in both the organizational and state-society arenas. The gap or "vacuum" that existed in state-society relations was also related to the organizational development of a state that had traditionally been distant and authoritarian. Although Sendero's activity was diminished by the state reforms of the early 1990s, permanently closing the state-society gap remained the major challenge to ensure social peace and the development of a more democratic and stable political order.

Notes

1. Timothy Wickham-Crowley, "Comparative Sociology of Guerrilla Movements," in Susan Eckstein, ed., *Power and Popular Protest* (Berkeley: University of California Press, 1988), p. 168.

2. Many leftist observers suggested that terrorist attacks were part of an attempt to discredit them by the CIA, while rightists claimed that Sendero was the armed wing of the legal left. See José María Salcedo, "El Papel del Terrorismo y el Terrorismo de Papel," *QueHacer* 9, 1981, pp. 38–45; and Gustavo Gorritti, *Sendero: Historia de una Guerra Milenaria* (Lima: Apoyo, 1990).

3. The legal basis of these decrees is discussed in Diego García Sayán, *Estados de Excepción en la Región Andina* (Lima: Comisión Andina de Juristas, 1987).

4. Noel suggested that the legal left and Sendero were "all guilty of the same irresponsible opposition carried out against the government." *Actualidad Militar,* May 1983, p. 30.

5. The most reliable source for figures on violence in Peru during this period remains the two volumes of DESCO, *Violencia Política en el Perú: 1980–1988* (Lima: DESCO, 1989).

6. *Caretas*, September 12, 1983, p. 13.

7. See Chapter Two.

8. *Caretas*, March 26, 1984, p. 20.

9. The developmentalist approach is outlined in a number of articles appearing in the journal *Defensa Nacional*, a publication of the Centro de Altos Estudios Militares (CAEM), between 1982 and 1986. See CAEM, "El Proceso de la Política Nacional," *Defensa Nacional* 7, December 1982, pp. 12–17.

10. See the interview with the new commander of the army, General Julián Julía, in *QueHacer* 34, April 1985, p. 11.

11. A dramatization of these events is found in Guillermo Thorndike, *La Revolución Imposible* (Lima: EMI, 1988).

12. A collection of important documents regarding the prison massacre are found in Juan Cristobal, *Todos Murieron?* (Lima: Terra Nueva, 1987).

13. See the interview with General Jorge Flores Torres in *QueHacer* 47, June 1987, p. 36. Also see *Actualidad Militar,* November 1985, p. 25.

14. Fernando Mattos, "Economía de Guerra Para el Ejército?" *Debate,* September 1989, p. 32.

15. *Sí,* June 9, 1991, p. 15.

16. The most explosive case involved the commander of the air force, General Germán Vucetich, who, among other things, was tied to a money laundering scheme. *Caretas,* May 28, 1990, p. 38.

17. *Caretas,* October 16, 1989, p. 32.

18. A comprehensive study of the Comando Rodrigo Franco was done by a special senate commission. See its final report in Senado de la República (Peru), *Informe de la Comisión Investigadora de Grupos Paramilitares* (Lima: República Peruana, 1990).

19. On individual cases, the reports issued by the human rights organization Americas Watch have been excellent sources for the activities and organization of paramilitary groups in the region. On El Salvador, see *A Year of Reckoning: El Salvador a Decade After the Assasination of Archbishop Romero* (New York: Human Rights Watch, 1990).

20. *La República,* June 5, 1987, p. 14.

21. The two most notable cases of the early 1990s involved a massacre of suspected Sendero sympathizers in the Barrios Altos section of Lima and the kidnapping and extrajudicial killing of university students and a professor from the Universidad La Cantuta in Lima. There was significant evidence, including testimony from a high ranking military officer forced out of the country, General Rodolfo Robles, that the army command knew of and sanctioned paramilitary activities. *Caretas,* May 10, 1993, pp. 10–16.

22. *Caretas,* August 6, 1990, p. 12.

23. See Marcial Rubio, "Pacificación o Lucha Contrasubversiva?" *QueHacer* 74, November 1991, pp. 5–10.

24. A first-hand account of the development and growth of the Cajamarca *rondas* is found in Antonio Ramírez, ed., *A Propósito de la Autodefensa de las Masas: Rondas Campesinas* (Chota-Cajamarca: Federación Departamental de Rondas Campesinas, 1986).

25. For a good overview of the *rondas* see Orin Starn, *Reflexiones Sobre Rondas Campesinas, Protesta Rural y Nuevos Movimientos Sociales* (Lima: Instituto de Estudios Peruanos, 1991).

26. A review of these problems and the debates surrounding the *rondas* in this period is found in Instituto de Defensa Legal, *Perú 1990* (Lima: IDL, 1991), pp. 135–139.

27. Orin Starn, "Sendero, Soldados y Ronderos en el Mantaro," *QueHacer* 74, November 1991, p. 61.

9

Conclusions:
From State Developmentalism
to Neoliberal Reforms

This study began with an examination of the Velasco developmentalist program and ended with the Fujimori regime's neoliberal reforms. Velasco and Fujimori were both political outsiders to the traditional elite structure; both were called "el chino" by their followers; and both introduced the most sweeping structural reforms in recent Peruvian history. Nonetheless, they stand at opposite ends of the recent cycle of state development and politics in Peru. In the interval, Peru experienced a series of dramatic social and economic dislocations that reshaped the state and state-society relations. Although the pace and scope of change varied, this shift from developmentalism to neoliberal reforms occurred elsewhere in Latin America during this period. State development in Peru since 1968 points to the importance of state power in this transition.

Specific economic and social policies were pursued by a series of authoritarian and democratic regimes with differing ideological agendas. State capabilities were substantially reduced over nearly a two decade period. Both the developmentalist policies of the 1970s and the neoliberal reforms of the early 1980s were implemented in ways that reduced the effectiveness of state activities. Most of these policies were adopted without sufficient political support, resources, planning, or organization. Moreover, diverse regimes tended to design and implement their policies with ideological rather than technical criteria guiding them. The result was a gradual decline in the efficacy of state institutions. Only during the Fujimori and Velasco regimes was the state able to avoid some of these pitfalls and, thus, enhance its capabilities. The analysis of those capabili-

ties focused on the three arenas of state power discussed in Chapter One and summarized below.

The State Organizational Arena

Much of this study has evaluated the changing organization and resources of the state. Two specific sets of capabilities were most directly weakened during the period studied. The first was the state's ability to regulate the economy through fiscal and monetary policies. Chapters Two and Three examined how the state increasingly lost control of its ability to maintain sufficient revenue in the face of domestic political pressures and its international debt obligations. Both of these pressures were in part the result of policies adopted during the Velasco period, especially state-directed mobilization and excessive borrowing on international markets. Moreover, tax revenue declined precipitously, public enterprise deficits soared, and the overall effectiveness of state agencies was reduced by corruption and populist practices. A second set of organizational capabilities related to internal order. During the Velasco regime, the armed forces grew increasingly divided over the issue of its own mobilization policies. Though such divisions were temporarily resolved with the removal of Velasco, they resurfaced in less than a decade over counterinsurgency. As we saw in Chapter Eight, persistent conflicts combined with economic pressures, corruption, and institutional rigidities, reduced the effectiveness of security forces.

Organizational capabilities were particularly amenable to reform by the Fujimori regime. Most of the neoliberal reforms discussed in Chapter Five were directed toward restructuring the state's organization, from the overhaul of the tax system and privatizations to the reorganization of the intelligence service. The rapid success of the reforms was possible, at least in part, by the coalition of national and international actors that the regime forged. This coalition provided the essential political support needed to overcome the institutional and social resistance encountered.

The International Arena

The state's vulnerability in the international arena resulted from changes beyond its control in the structure of international economic power. The growing importance of financial and commercial capitalism within the international economic structure left many Third World states, such as Peru, particularly vulnerable. The international debt contracted during the 1970s and early 1980s resulted in a clear loss of decision-making power by the Peruvian state to international financial agencies and private foreign banks. Policies adopted to regain leverage during the

García administration failed dramatically and left the country in an even more precarious and vulnerable position than it had been as a primary product exporter. The changes brought about by the Fujimori regime during the early 1990s had little immediate impact on the state's position in the international arena, given the importance of international financial actors in the Fujimori coalition.

The State-Society Arena

In the wake of the collapse of Velasco's mobilization project, the state confronted an unprecedented level of organization in civil society. Popular sector organizations demonstrated a persistent willingness to challenge state authority and prerogatives, demonstrated by the dramatic rise in strikes and social protests after the mid-1970s. The degree to which the mobilization project reshaped society in unexpected ways was discussed in Chapters Six and Seven. Both Villa El Salvador and Sendero Luminoso owed their existence in part to the reforms introduced under Velasco. Although Villa represented the hopes of progressives in the regime and Sendero represented the regime's fears, the development of both underlined the unintended consequences of state policies in society. By the late 1980s the state's ability to influence and organize social groups was highly limited. The rapid spread of insurgency suggested that the state was also having difficulty maintaining its legitimacy among significant social sectors. While the Fujimori reforms of the early 1990s attempted to reverse this situation, it probably will be several years before their full impact can be assessed.

The focus on the three arenas of state power provided a clear illustration of how state capabilities in one area can influence capabilities in other areas. In Peru, external vulnerabilities regarding the debt had dire consequences for the state's organizational capacities, that in turn weakened the ability of the state to influence societal actors. Declining state influence in the societal arena contributed to the emergence of new social actors willing to challenge state prerogatives, that in turn presented new threats to the state's organizational capacities.

One of the most important implications that can be drawn from the analysis of this book concerns the role of policy. In each of the arenas discussed, the crisis of state power resulted from specific choices made by policy makers. The consequences of most of these decisions were unforeseen. Many of the key decisions were taken by officials with little or no understanding of the structural limitations they were facing. Both the military's mobilization policies of the 1970s and its counterinsurgency strategies of the 1980s vastly overestimated the state's ability to penetrate and reorganize society, particularly rural society, while maintaining legitimacy. In both instances, military planners failed to build a consensus among affected actors about policy goals or to even communicate effectively with them. As a result, potential allies were alienated or became part of the opposition. The same pattern regarding structural obstacles and potential allies can be found when examining economic policy making. From the Velasco to the García period, those responsible for the economy vastly underestimated Peru's external vulnerabilities and overestimated domestic economic performance. The choices based on these erroneous assumptions significantly worsened what were already difficult economic situations. Moreover, economic policy making was often based on ideological configurations that did not correspond to reality. The rigidity of this approach, as demonstrated in the Morales and Belaúnde policy toward labor or the García bank nationalization, tended to raise the level of social conflict and isolate policy makers.

Neither ideological orientation nor political regime appeared to significantly affect the deterioration of state capabilities in Peru. In the period examined, Peru was governed by authoritarian military regimes and civilian democratic regimes. Similarly, the dominant ideology of the regimes during this period also varied. While the Morales, Belaúnde, and Fujimori regimes were decidedly neoliberal and conservative, the Velasco and García regimes were leftist and populist. Our analysis suggested that the state crisis in Peru was more often than not linked to the way policies were implemented and goals defined. Overly ambitious and unrealistic goals that failed to take into account the real capabilities of the state did considerable damage. Policy makers often appeared to think that the state was capable of doing almost anything, from organizing political society to redirecting the economy in the short-term, to changing the structure of Peru's international position. Policies were often adopted without sufficient support within the state itself or from affected groups. This laid the groundwork for conflicts that reduced the efficacy of the policies being pursued. To a large extent these shortcomings were driven by short-term political calculation or an unwillingness to compromise ideological preconceptions.

Although many supporters of neoliberal reforms suggested that the multiple crises affecting the state during the 1970s and 1980s were the direct result of the developmentalist model, this study does not support that conclusion. Policy success appeared to be linked more closely to political support, resource availability, the international environment, planning, and organization, than to the particular ideological program involved. The failures of neoliberal experiments carried out during the Morales and Belaúnde regimes stand as clear reminders that a successful outcome for neoliberalism was neither inherent nor inevitable. The initial successes of the Velasco and Fujimori reform programs, though vastly different in conception and orientation, depended on the crucial factors mentioned above rather than on the ideology of their programs and followers.

A related conclusion with comparative ramifications is that the transition from developmentalism to neoliberalism did not involve a smooth and linear progression. Rather, for over two decades the policies adopted by the Peruvian state swung between these models, and, indeed, during the late 1980s, elements of both models were being implemented simultaneously. This "zigzag" approach largely resulted from shifting political coalitions and international pressures.[1] High levels of political mobilization among the popular classes created new demands on the state's resources, while international actors became involved in domestic policy making to an unprecedented degree. The greater stability of the Fujimori administration's neoliberalism illustrated the importance of both political support and the international environment. That regime successfully avoided dramatic swings in policy due to the strength of the political coalition behind reforms and the international circumstances favorable to these reforms during the early 1990s.

Peru's state development since the early 1970s paralleled trends in state development elsewhere in Latin America. While this is not the place to engage in detailed comparisons, it is worth noting some of the broader comparative issues raised by the framework of state power used here. The declining efficacy of the state, growing vulnerabilities to international financial institutions, and dramatic changes in state-society relations, were problems many Latin American countries shared.

The declining efficacy of state institutions throughout the region originated in the economic crisis that turned the 1980s into the "lost decade" for most countries. But as with Peru, the impact of the economic crisis on the state resulted in more than a simple reduction of revenue and resources.[2] The state's organizational capabilities were affected by the inevitable corruption, the loss of qualified personnel in state bureaucracies, and rising social protests. To respond to the crisis, regimes in such countries as Venezuela, Brazil, and Argentina, also confronted some of the same policy making difficulties and limitations their counterparts in Peru encountered. The difficulties that developed as a result of the various "heterodox" experiments of the mid-1980s suggested that problems in state planning and organization were compounded by shifting and unstable political coalitions and assertive international financial actors.[3]

As the economic crisis of the late 1970s deepened during the 1980s, it became apparent that an important change had occurred in the role international financial actors played. The onset of the debt crisis in Latin America was accompanied by an extraordinary level of outside intervention, both direct and indirect, in the management of state policy. The IMF, World Bank, foreign governments, and private foreign banks, became important actors in shaping domestic policy throughout the region by breaking down the traditional boundaries of domestic and international influence.[4] Arguably, the vulnerability of Latin America's largest debtors to the pressure and influence of international banks and financial agencies represented a mere shift in the type of dependency that had traditionally structured the relation between the states of the region and the international capitalist system. In previous decades international actors used their influence through commodity markets, trading arrangements, and gunboat diplomacy. The 1980s witnessed growing foreign influence in central banks, stock markets, and finance ministries. The globalization of international capital brought about by rapid technological changes and a redistribution of production made the international arena crucial in shaping state capabilities. While dependency theory is useful in understanding these changes, renewed theory and research on the relationship between state development and the new global economy are needed.

Finally, many of the changes in state-society relations in Peru also have important parallels elsewhere in Latin America. Foremost among these has been the ability of new social movements to challenge state domination. New social movements, especially among the poor, have made it more difficult, although not impossible, for state elites to create the type of corporatist or clientelist systems traditionally used to dominate popular sector actors.[5] From Brazil to Mexico, new social movements have empowered the poor and led to new organizations autonomous from state control. Yet as we saw throughout this book, the state-society relation is complex and not zero-sum. Neoliberal reforms during the 1990s in the region stressed a strengthening of state penetration of society. This was especially prominent under the Salinas administration in Mexico, which invested heavily in new social programs that were thinly veiled attempts to counter the growing influence of autonomous popular institutions.[6]

The wave of democratization in Latin America from the 1980s onward also had important implications for state-society relations. Democracy implied a vigorous civil society and clear rules of interaction among social groups and between civil society and the state. Given that much of the traditional dominance of the state in Latin America relied upon authoritarian methods, this change has serious implications. Respect for the autonomy of society and clear rules of interaction can provide for longer-term stability as both state and societal actors develop routine interactions through the rules and institutions of political democracy. The case of Peru under Fujimori also demonstrated that nothing is inevitable about this process. When the Fujimori regime became frustrated over its inability to reform the state through democratic procedures and norms, it discarded them.

As Peru and Latin America continue the neoliberal reforms begun since the late 1980s, the role of the state is likely to continue changing dramatically. The direction of those changes, as this study has suggested, will depend on a variety of factors over that policy makers often have little influence. The discourse of neoliberalism berates the state's role in the economy and society. Yet if the case of Peru is indicative, the reforms of the early 1990s may have the ironic effect of strengthening the power and influence of the state in society.

Notes

1. A similar conclusion was reached by Frieden in his comparative analysis, though Frieden discounts the importance of international factors. Jeffrey Frieden, *Debt, Development and Democracy: Modern Political Economy and Latin America, 1965–1985* (Princeton: Princeton University Press, 1991).

2. An interesting discussion of the relation between the economic crisis and the state in Latin America is found in Guillermo O'Donnell, "The State, Democratization and Some Conceptual Problems," in William Smith, Carlos Acuña and Eduardo Gamarra, eds., *Latin American Political Economy in the Age of Neoliberalism* (New Brunswick: Transaction Press, 1993), pp. 157–179.

3. See Barbara Stallings and Robert Kaufman, eds., *Debt and Democracy in Latin America* (Boulder: Westview Press, 1989).

4. See Barbara Stallings, "International Influence on Economic Policy: Debt, Stabilization and Structural Reforms," in Stephen Haggard and Robert Kaufman, eds., *The Politics of Economic Adjustment* (Princeton: Princeton University Press, 1992), pp. 41–88.

5. See especially, Arturo Escobar and Sonia Alvarez, eds., *The Making of Social Movements in Latin America* (Boulder: Westview Press, 1992).

6. On the Salinas reforms and their social costs see Nora Lustig, *Mexico: The Remaking of an Economy* (Washington D.C: Brookings Institution, 1992).

Selected Bibliography

Books, Articles and Documents

Adrianzén, Alberto. 1991. "Y la Oposición, Donde Esta?" *QueHacer* 70: 10–13.

Alarcón, Germán. 1991. "Modernización o Retroceso?" *QueHacer* 74: 14–15.

Alberti, Giorgio, Jorge Santiestevan, and Luis Pasara. 1977. *La Comunidad Industrial en el Perú.* Lima: Instituto de Estudios Peruanos.

Allou, Serge. 1989. *Lima en Letras.* Lima: CIDAP-IFEA.

Americas Watch. 1984. *Abdicating Democratic Authority.* New York: Americas Watch.

———. 1988. *Tolerancia Frente los Abusos.* Lima: Comisión Andina de Juristas.

———. 1990. *A Year of Reckoning: El Salvador a Decade After the Assassination of Archbishop Romero.* New York: Americas Watch.

Aragón, Antonio. 1983. "La CUAVES: Un Simbolo, una Esperanza," in CELADEC, ed., *Villa El Salvador: De Arenal a Distrito Municipal.* Pp. 1–36. Lima: CELADEC.

Ardant, Gabriel. 1975. "Financial Policy and Economic Infrastructure of Modern States and Nations," in Charles Tilly, ed., *The Formation of National States in Western Europe.* Pp. 164–242. Princeton: Princeton University Press.

Arriagada, Genaro. n.d. *El Pensamiento Político de los Militares: Estudios Sobre Chile, Argentina, Brasil y Uruguay.* Santiago: Centro de Investigaciones Socioeconomicos.

Balbi, Carmen Rosa. 1987. "Sindicalismo y Caminos de Concertación." *Socialismo y Participación* 38: 77–93.

———. 1989. *Identidad Clasista en el Sindicalismo.* Lima: DESCO.

———. 1989. "Estrategias Obreras: La Recesión Silenciosa." *QueHacer* 59: 12–22.

Becker, David. 1981. *The New Bourgeoisie and the Limits of Dependency: Mining, Class and Power in 'Revolutionary' Peru.* Princeton: Princeton University Press.

Berg, Ronald. 1987. "Sendero Luminoso and the Peasantry of Andahuaylas." *Journal of Inter-American and World Affairs* 28, no. 4 (Winter 1986–87): 164–197.

Bermeo, Nancy, ed., 1992. *Liberalization and Democratization: Change in the Soviet Union and Eastern Europe.* Baltimore: Johns Hopkins University Press.

Bernales, Enrique. 1987. *Socialismo y Nación.* Lima: Mesa Redonda.

Blondet, Cecilia. 1991. *Las Mujeres y el Poder: Una Historia de Villa El Salvador.* Lima: Instituto de Estudios Peruanos.

Bourricaud, Francois. 1970. *Power and Society in Contemporary Peru.* New York: Praeger Publishers.

Burga, Jorge, and Claire Delpech. 1989. *Villa El Salvador: La Ciudad y su Desarollo.* Lima: CIED.

Burga, Manuel. 1971. *De la Encomienda a la Hacienda Capitalista.* Lima: Instituto de Estudios Peruanos.

Burga, Manuel, and Alberto Flores Galindo. 1980. *Apogeo y Crisis de la República Aristocrática.* Lima: Editorial Rikchay.

Calderón, Julio, and Luis Olivera. 1979. *Manual del Poblador de Pueblos Jóvenes.* Lima: DESCO.

Callaghey, Thomas. 1984. *The State-Society Struggle: Zaire in Comparative Perspective.* New York: Columbia University Press.

Cameron, Maxwell. 1994. *Democracy and Authoritarianism in Peru.* New York: St. Martins Press.

Carbonetto, Daniel. 1987. *Un Modelo Económico Heterodoxo: El Caso Peruano.* Lima: Instituto Nacional de Planificación.

Carnoy, Martin. 1987. *The State and Political Theory.* Princeton: Princeton University Press.

Centro de Altos Estudios Militares (CAEM). 1982. "El Proceso de la Política Nacional." *Defensa Nacional* 7: 13–17.

Centro de Estudios Cristianos y Capacitación Popular (CECYCAP). n.d. *Comedores Familiares: Manual de Organización, Roles y Funciones.* Arequipa: CECYCAP.

Centro Latinoamericano de Trabajo Social (CELATS). 1983. *Manual de Organización y Funciones de los Comedores Populares de El Agustino.* Lima: CELATS.

Chávez, Eliana. 1990. "El Empleo en los Sectores Populares," in Alberto Busatamante, ed., *De Marginales a Informales.* Pp. 71–124. Lima: DESCO.

Chávez de Paz, Dennis. 1989. *Juventud y Terrorismo.* Lima: Instituto de Estudios Peruanos.

Chirinos, Luis A. 1986. "Gobierno Local y Participación Vecinal: El Caso de Lima Metropolitana." *Socialismo y Participación* 36: 1–27.

Collier, David. 1976. *Squatters and Oligarchs.* Baltimore: Johns Hopkins University Press.

———. 1978. *The New Authoritarianism in Latin America.* Princeton: Princeton University Press.

Comité de Coordinación y Unificación Sindical Clasista (CCUSC). 1976. "Conclusiones y Resoluciones." Lima: CCUSC.

Comunidad Urbana Autogestionario de Villa El Salvador (CUAVES). 1984. *Villa El Salvador: Un Pueblo Una Realidad.* Lima: CUAVES.

———. 1986. "Acta de Compromiso y Acatamiento de las Listas de Candidatos al Concejo Distrital Frente a la CUAVES." Lima: CUAVES.

Confederación Campesina del Perú (CCP). 1974. "Plataforma de Lucha." Lima: CCP.

Confederación General de Trabajadores del Perú (CGTP). 1972. "Los Sindicatos y el Area Laboral de SINAMOS." Lima: CGTP.

———. 1978. "Mayo 22–23: Testimonio de la CGTP." Lima: CGTP.

———. 1978. "Documentos: V Congreso." Lima: CGTP.

Conniff, Michael. 1982. *Latin American Populism in Comparative Perspective.* Albuquerque: University of New Mexico Press.

Cotler, Julio. 1970. "The Mechanics of Internal Domination and Social Change in Peru," in Irving Louis Horowitz, ed., *Masses in Latin America*. Pp. 407–444. New York: Oxford University Press.

————. 1978. *Clases, Estado y Nación*. Lima: Instituto de Estudios Peruanos.

————. 1994. *Política y Sociedad en el Perú*. Lima: Instituto de Estudios Peruanos.

Cristobal, Juan. 1987. *Todos Murieron?* Lima: Editores Tierra Nueva.

Dancourt, Oscar. 1989. "Sobre la Hyperinflación Peruana." *Economía* 12: 13–44.

Degregori, Carlos Iván. 1990. *El Surgimiento de Sendero Luminoso: Ayacucho, 1969–1979*. Lima: Instituto de Estudios Peruanos.

Degregori, Carlos Iván, and Romeo Grompone. 1991. *Elecciones 1990: Demonios y Redentores en el Nuevo Perú*. Lima: Instituto de Estudios Peruanos.

Delgado, Carlos. 1974. *El Proceso Revolucionario Peruano: Testimonio de Lucha.* Mexico D.F.: Siglo XXI.

Del Pilar Tello, María. 1983. *Golpe o Revolución?* (2 Volumes). Lima: SAGSA.

Del Prado, Jorge. 1987. *Cuatro Facetas de la Historia del PCP*. Lima: Ediciones Unidad.

DESCO. 1977. *Cronología Política 1976*. Lima: DESCO.

————. 1978. *Cronología Política 1977*. Lima: DESCO.

————. 1979. *Cronología Política 1978*. Lima: DESCO.

————. 1989. *Violencia Política en el Perú: 1980–1988*. Lima: DESCO.

DeSoto, Hernando. 1986. *El Otro Sendero*. Lima: El Barranco.

Dietz, Henry. 1980. *Poverty and Problem Solving Under Military Rule.* Austin: University of Texas Press.

DiTella, Torcuato. 1965. "Populism and Reform in Latin America," in Claudio Velíz, ed., *Obstacles to Change in Latin America*. Pp. 47–74. London: Oxford University Press.

Dobyns, Henry and Paul Doughty. 1976. *Peru: A Cultural History.* Oxford: Oxford University Press.

Durand, Francisco. 1994. *Business and Politics in Peru*. Boulder: Westview Press.

Eckstein, Susan. 1983. "Revolution and Redistribution," in Cynthia McClintock and Abraham Lowenthal, eds., *The Peruvian Experiment Reconsidered*. Pp. 347–386. Princeton: Princeton University Press.

Escobar, Arturo, and Sonia Alvarez, eds., 1992. *The Making of Social Movements in Latin America*. Boulder: Westview Press.

Evans, Peter, Dietrich Reuschmeyer, and Theda Skocpol, eds., 1985. *Bringing the State Back In*. New York: Cambridge University Press.

Favre, Henri. 1984. "Perú: Sendero Luminoso y Horizontes Oscuros." *QueHacer* 31: 25–35.

Fitzgerald, E.V.K. 1983. "State Capitalism in Peru," in Cynthia McClintock and Abraham Lowenthal, eds., *The Peruvian Experiment Reconsidered*. Pp. 65–93. Princeton: Princeton University Press.

Flores Galindo, Alberto. 1987. *Buscando un Inca*. Lima: Instituto de Apoyo Agraria.

Frieden, Jeffrey. 1991. *Debt, Development and Democracy: Modern Political Economy and Latin America: 1965–1985*. Princeton: Princeton University Press.

Fuenzalida, Fernando, Enrique Mayer, Francois Bourricaud. 1970. *El Indio y el Poder en el Perú*. Lima: Instituto de Estudios Peruanos.

Galler, Nora and Pilar Nuñez. 1989. *Mujer y Comedor Popular*. Lima: SEPADE.

Gamero, Julio. 1988. "Cómo y Porqué se Gestó la Crisis: Del Shock Heterodoxo al Ajuste Ortodoxo." *QueHacer* 55: 15–17.

García Pérez, Alan. 1987. *El Futuro Diferente: La Tarea Historica del APRA*. 2nd Edition, Lima: EMI.

García Sayan, Diego. 1982. *Las Tomas de Tierra en el Perú*. Lima: DESCO.

———. 1987. *Estados de Excepción en la Región Andina*. Lima: Comisión Andina de Juristas.

Gerth H., and C. Wright Mills. 1958. *From Max Weber*. New York: Oxford University Press.

Gonzalez, Raúl. 1986. "Qué Pasa en Puno?" *QueHacer* 43: 41–52.

———. 1988. "MRTA: La Historia Desconocida." *QueHacer* 51: 32–44.

Gonzáles de Olarte, Efraín. 1989. *Economía para la Democracia*. Lima: Instituto de Estudios Peruanos.

Gorritti, Gustavo. 1990. *Sendero Luminoso: Historia de la Guerra Milenaria en el Perú*. Lima: Apoyo.

Graham, Carol. 1992. *Peru's APRA: Parties, Politics and the Elusive Quest for Democracy*. Boulder: Lynne Reinner.

Granados, Manuel. 1987. "El PCP-SL: Approximación a su Ideologia." *Socialismo y Participación* 37: 17–31

Grindle, Merilee. 1986. *State and Countryside: Development and Agrarian Policy in Latin America*. Baltimore: Johns Hopkins Press.

Guasti, Laura. 1983. "The Peruvian Military Government and International Corporations," in Cynthia McClintock and Abraham Lowenthal, eds., *The Peruvian Experiment Reconsidered*. Pp. 181–204. Princeton: Princeton University Press.

Gurr, Ted Robert. 1970. *Why Men Rebel*. Princeton: Princeton University Press.

Hamilton, Nora. 1982. *The Limits of State Autonomy: Post-Revolutionary Mexico*. Princeton: Princeton University Press.

Haya de la Torre, Victor Raúl. 1986. *El Anti-Imperialismo y El APRA*. Lima: APRA.

———. 1986. *Treinta Años de Aprismo*. Lima: APRA.

Hobsbawm, Eric. 1990. *Nations and Nationalism Since 1780*. New York: Cambridge University Press.

Hudson, Michael. 1977. *Arab Politics*. New Haven: Yale University Press.

Huntington, Samuel. 1968. *Political Order in Changing Societies*. New Haven: Yale University Press.

Instituto de Defensa Legal. 1988. *Los Derechos Humanos y su Protección Legal*. Lima: IDL.

———. 1990. *Perú 1989: En la Espiral de la Violencia*. Lima: IDL.

———. 1991. *Perú 1990: La Oportunidad Perdida*. Lima: IDL.

Instituto Nacional de Estadísticas (INE). 1987. *Compendio Estadístico 1986*. Lima: República Peruana.

International Labour Organization (ILO). 1970. *Yearbook of Labour Statistics*. Volume 30. Geneva: ILO.

———. 1975. *Yearbook of Labour Statistics*. Volume 35. Geneva: ILO.

———. 1980. *Yearbook of Labour Statistics*. Volume 40. Geneva: ILO.

Izquierda Unida (IU). 1985. *Documentos Fundamentales de la Izquierda Unida*. Lima: IU.

Jochamovitz, Luis. 1993. *Ciudadano Fujimori: La Construcción de un Político.* Lima: PEISA.

Johnson, Chalmers. 1972. *Ideology and Politics in Contemporary China.* Seattle: University of Washington Press.

Kisic, Drago. 1987. *De la Corresponsabilidad a la Moratoria: El Caso de la Deuda Peruana, 1970–1986.* Lima: Friedrich Ebert.

Klaiber, Jeffrey. 1988. *La Iglesia en el Perú.* Lima: Universidad Católica.

Kruijt, Dirk. 1990. *Revolución Por Decreto.* Lima: Mosca Azul.

Lago, Ricardo. 1991. "The Illusion of Pursuing Redistribution Through Macropolicy: Peru's Heterodox Experience, 1985–1990," in Rudiger Dornbusch and Sebastian Edwards, eds., *The Macroeconomics of Populism in Latin America.* Pp. 263–330. Chicago: University of Chicago Press.

Letts, Ricardo. 1981. *La Izquierda Peruana.* Lima: Mosca Azul.

Lowenthal, Abraham. 1975. *The Peruvian Experiment.* Princeton: Princeton University Press.

Lustig, Nora. 1993. *Mexico: The Remaking of an Economy.* Washington D.C.: Brookings Institution.

Lynch, Nicolás. 1990. *Los Jóvenes Rojos de San Marcos: El Radicalismo Universitario de los Años Setenta.* Lima: El Zorro de Abajo.

Malia, Martin. 1992. "Leninist Endgame." *Daedalus* 121, no. 2: 57–75.

Malloy, James, ed., 1978. *Authoritarianism and Corporatism in Latin America.* Pittsburgh: University of Pittsburgh Press.

Manrique, Nelson. 1988. *Yawar Mayu.* Lima: DESCO.

———. 1990. "Política y Violencia en el Perú." *Margenes* 5: 137–182.

Mao Tse-tung. 1966. *The Collected Works of Mao Tse-tung.* Peking: Foreign Language Press.

Masterson, Daniel. 1991. *Militarism and Politics in Latin America: Peru From Sánchez Cerro to Sendero Luminoso.* Westport: Greenwood Press.

Matos Mar, José, and José Manuel Mejía. 1980. *La Reforma Agraria en el Perú.* Lima: Instituto de Estudios Peruanos.

Mattos, F. 1989. "Economía de Guerra para el Ejército?" *Debate.* (September): 32–34.

Mauceri, Philip. 1991. "Military Politics and Counterinsurgency in Peru." *Journal of Inter-American and World Affairs* 33: 83–109.

———. 1995. "State Reform, Coalitions, and the Neoliberal Autogolpe in Peru." *Latin American Research Review* 30: 7–37.

McClintock, Cynthia. 1981. *Peasant Cooperatives and Political Change in Peru.* Princeton: Princeton University Press.

———. 1983. *The Peruvian Experiment Reconsidered.* Princeton: Princeton University Press.

———. 1984. "Why Peasants Rebel: The Case of Peru's Sendero Luminoso." *World Politics* 37: 48–84.

———. 1989. "The Prospects for Democratization in a Least Likely Case: Peru." *Comparative Politics* 2: 127–148.

Mesnier, Maurice. 1974. "Utopian Socialist Themes in Maoism," in John L. Lewis, ed., *Peasant Rebellion and Communist Revolution in Asia.* Pp. 207–252. Stanford: Stanford University Press.

Migdal, Joel. 1988. *Strong Societies and Weak States*. Princeton: Princeton University Press.

Migdal, Joel, Atul Kohli, and Vivienne Shue, eds., 1994. *State Power and Social Forces: Domination and Transformation in the Third World*. Cambridge: Cambridge University Press.

Moncloa, Francisco. 1980. "La Constitución, el APRA y el Nuevo Modelo de Dependencia." *Cuadernos Socialistas* 3: 12–24.

Nelson, Joan, ed., 1990. *Economic Crisis and Policy Choices: The Politics of Adjustment in the Third World*. Princeton: Princeton University Press.

Nettl, J.P. 1968. "The State as a Conceptual Variable." *World Politics* 20: 559–592.

Nieto, Jorge. 1983. *Izquierda y Democracia en el Perú: 1975–1980*. Lima: DESCO.

O'Donnell, Guillermo, Philippe Schmitter and Laurence Whitehead. 1985. *Transitions From Authoritarian Rule: Tentative Conclusions About Uncertain Outcomes*. Baltimore: Johns Hopkins University Press.

———. 1994. "The State, Democratization and Some Conceptual Problems," in William Smith, Carlos Acuña, and Eduardo Gamarra, eds., *Latin American Political Economy in the Age of Neoliberal Reform*. Pp. 157–180. New Brunswick: Transaction Press.

Panfichi, Aldo. 1983. "La Crisis y las Multitudes: Lima, 5 de Febrero de 1975." *Debates en Sociología* 9: 31–64.

Paredes C., Peri. 1988. "La Instrumentalización Política del PAIT." Unpublished manuscript. Lima.

Paredes, Carlos, and Jeffrey Sachs. 1991. *Peru's Path to Recovery: A Plan For Economic Stabilization and Growth*. Washington D.C.: Brookings Institution.

Paredes Macedo, Saturnino. 1968. *Acerca de la Historia del Partido y sus Luchas*. Lima: Ediciones Bandera Roja.

———. 1986. *Los Sindicatos Clasistas y sus Principios*. Lima: CESEP.

Parodi, Jorge. 1986. *La Desmovilización del Sindicalismo Industrial Peruano Durante el Segundo Belaundismo*. Lima: Instituto de Estudios Peruanos.

Pásara, Luis. 1987. *Radicalización y Conflicto en la Iglesia Peruana*. Lima: El Virrey.

Pásara, Luis, and Jorge Parodi, eds., 1988. *Democracia, Sociedad y Gobierno en el Perú*. Lima: CEDYS.

Partido Aprista Peruana (PAP). 1975. "Comunicado del PAP Sobre los Sucesos del 5 de Febrero." Lima: PAP.

Partido Comunista del Peru-Bandera Roja (PCP-BR). 1965. "Conclusiones y Resoluciones de la V Congreso Nacional del PCP." Lima: Ediciones Bandera Roja.

Partido Comunista del Peru-Sendero Luminoso (PCP-SL). 1982. "Desarollemos la Guerra de Guerrilleras." Lima: PCP-SL.

———. 1986. "Desarollar la Guerra Popular Sirviendo a la Revolución." Lima: PCP-SL.

———. 1988. "Documentos Fundamentales del Primer Congreso del Partido Comunista del Perú." Lima: PCP-SL.

———. 1989. "Sobre el Comité Popular." Lima: PCP-SL.

Partido Comunista Peruana (PCP). 1979. "Conclusiones y Resoluciones del VII Congreso Nacional." Lima: PCP.

Pastor, Manuel, and Carol Wise. 1992. "Peruvian Economic Policy in the 1980s." *Latin American Research Review* 27: 83–117.

Pease García, Henry. 1981. *Los Caminos del Poder.* Lima: DESCO.

———. 1986. *El Ocaso del Poder Oligárquico.* Lima: DESCO.

———. 1987. "El Populismo Aprista: Ni Reformas, ni Revolución." *QueHacer* 47: 44–50.

———. 1988. *Democracia y Precariedad Bajo el Populismo Aprista.* Lima: DESCO.

Poole, Deborah, and Gerardo Renique. 1991. "The New Chroniclers of Peru: US Scholars and their 'Shining Path' of Peasant Rebellion." *Bulletin of Latin American Research* 10, no. 2: 133–191.

Portocarrero, Felipe. 1980. *Crisis y Recuperación.* Lima: Mosca Azul.

Quintanilla, Lino. 1981. *Andahuaylas: La Lucha por la Tierra.* Lima: Mosca Azul.

Ramos Tremolada, Ricardo. 1988. "El APRA en Vísperas de su XVI Congreso." *QueHacer* 53: 24–33.

Reich, Walter, ed., 1990. *Origins of Terrorism: Psychologies, Ideologies, States of Mind.* Cambridge: Cambridge University.

Reid, Michael. 1985. *Peru: Paths to Poverty.* London: Latin American Bureau.

Renique, José Luis. 1986. "Democracia y Movimiento Social en el Sur Andino," in Eduardo Ballon, ed., *Movimientos Sociales y Democracia.* Pp. 185–228. Lima: DESCO.

———. 1987. "Estado, Partido y Lucha por la Tierra en Puno." *Debate Agrario* 1: 55–76.

Rice, Edward. 1972. *Mao's Way.* Berkeley: University of California Press.

Rochabrun, Guillermo. 1988. "Izquierda, Democracia y Crisis en el Perú." *Margenes* 3: 79–99.

Rockman, Bert. 1990. "Minding the State—Or a State of Mind? Issues in the Comparative Conceptualization of the State." *Comparative Political Studies* 23: 25–55.

Rojas Julca, Julio Andrés. 1986. *Gobierno Municipal y Participación Ciudadana: Experiencias de Lima Metropolitana.* Lima: Friedrich Ebert.

Roncagliolo, Rafael. 1980. *Quien Ganó? Elecciones 1931–1980.* Lima: DESCO.

Rosenau, James. 1988. "The State in an Era of Cascading Politics." *Comparative Political Studies* 21: 13–44.

Rubio, Marcial. 1988. "La Danza de las Ilusiones." *Debate* 53: 8–10.

———. 1991. "Pacificación o Lucha Contrainsurgente?" *QueHacer* 74: 5–10.

Ruíz Caro, Ariela. 1990. "Reinserción: Cuentas de Nunca Acabar." *QueHacer* 73: 12–17.

Salcedo, José María. 1981. "El Papel del Terrorismo y el Terrorismo de Papel." *QueHacer* 9: 38–45.

———. 1995. *Terremoto: Cómo Ganó Fujimori?* Lima: Ediciones Brasa.

Sánchez, Rodrigo. 1982. *Tomas de Tierra y Conciencia Política Campesina.* Lima: Instituto de Estudios Peruanos.

Sartori, Giovanni. 1976. *Parties and Party Systems.* Cambridge: Cambridge University Press.

Schlydowsky, Daniel and Juan Wicht. 1979. *Anatomía de un Fracaso Económico: Perú 1968–1978.* Lima: CIUP.

Scott Palmer, David. 1973. *Revolution From Above: Military Government and Popular Participation in Peru.* Dissertation Series 47. Ithaca: Cornell University.

———. 1986. "Rebellion in Rural Peru: The Origins and Evolution of Sendero Luminoso." *Comparative Politics* 18: 127–146.

———, ed., 1992. *Shining Path of Peru*. New York: St. Martin's Press.

Senado de la República (Perú). 1988. *Violencia y Pacificación*. (3 Volumes). Lima: República Peruana.

———. 1990. *Informe de la Comisión Investigadora de Grupos Paramilitares*. Lima: Democracia y Socialismo.

Sistema Nacional de Apoyo a la Movilización Social (SINAMOS). n.d. "Características de la Revolución Peruana." Lima: SINAMOS.

———. n.d. "Los Grupos del Poder." Lima: SINAMOS.

———. n.d. "El Fenomeno Ultra." Lima: SINAMOS.

———. 1972. "SINAMOS: Sindicalismo." Lima: SINAMOS.

Skocpol, Theda. 1979. *States and Social Revolutions*. Cambridge: Cambridge University Press.

Slater, David. 1985. *New Social Movements and the State in Latin America*. Amsterdam: CEDLA.

Stallings, Barbara. 1983. "International Capitalism and the Peruvian Military Government, 1968–1978," in Cynthia McClintock and Abraham Lowenthal, eds., *The Peruvian Experiment Reconsidered*. Pp. 144–180. Princeton: Princeton University Press.

———. 1992. "International Influence on Economic Policy: Debt, Stabilization and Structural Reform," in Stephan Haggard and Robert Kaufman, eds., *The Political Economy of Adjustment*. Pp. 41–88. Princeton: Princeton University Press.

Starn, Orin. 1991. *Reflexiones Sobre las Rondas Campesinas, Protesta Rural y Nuevos Movimientos Sociales*. Lima: Instituto de Estudios Peruanos.

———. 1991. "Sendero, Soldados y Ronderos en el Mantaro." *QueHacer* 74: 60–68.

Starr, John Bryant. 1979. *Continuing the Revolution: The Political Thought of Mao Tsetung*. Princeton: Princeton University Press.

Stepan, Alfred. 1978. *State and Society: Peru in Comparative Perspective*. Princeton: Princeton University Press.

———. 1988. *Rethinking Military Politics*. Princeton: Princeton University Press.

Stokes, Susan. 1990. "Politics and Latin America's Urban Poor: Reflections From a Lima Shantytown." *Latin American Research Review* 26: 75–102.

Sulmont, Denis. 1985. *El Movimiento Obrero Peruano: 1890–1980*. Fifth Ed. Lima: Tarea.

Tarazona-Sevillano, Gabriela. 1991. *Sendero Luminoso and the Threat of NarcoTerrorism*. New York: Praeger Publishers.

Tarrow, Sidney. 1994. *Power in Movement: Social Movements, Collective Action and Politics*. Cambridge: Cambridge University Press.

Thorndike, Guillermo. 1976. *No, Mi General*. Lima: Mosca Azul.

———. 1988. *La Revolución Imposible*. Lima: EMI.

Thorp, Rosemary, and Geoffrey Bertram. 1978. *Growth and Policy in an Open Economy*. New York: Columbia University Press.

Tilly, Charles. 1978. *From Mobilization to Revolution*. New York: Random House Press.

Tovar, Teresa. 1982. *Movimiento Popular y Paros Nacionales*. Lima: DESCO.

Trimberger, Ellen Kay. 1978. *Revolution From Above: Military Bureaucrats and Development in Japan, Turkey, Egypt and Peru.* New Brunswick: Transaction Books.

Tuesta, Fernando. 1979. "Análisis del Proceso Electoral a la Asamblea Constituyente." Unpublished manuscript, Lima: Universidad Católica.

———. 1985. *El Nuevo Rostro Electoral: La Municipales del 83.* Lima: DESCO.

———. 1987. *Perú Política en Cifras.* Lima: Friedrich Ebert.

———. 1988. "Villa El Salvador: Izquierda, Gestión Municipal y Organización Popular." Unpublished manuscript, Lima.

———. 1989. *Pobreza Urbana y Cambios Electorales.* Lima: DESCO.

Unión Democratica Popular (UDP). 1978. "UDP: Balance y Tareas de la Unidad." Lima: UDP.

Valderrama, Mariano, ed., 1980. *El APRA: Un Camino de Esperanzas y Frustraciones.* Lima: El Gallo Rojo.

Valencia Quintanilla, Felix. 1984. *Luchas Campesinas en el Contexto Semi-Feudal del Oriente de Lucanas (Ayacucho).* Lima: CPEA.

Valenzuela, Arturo, and Samuel Valenzuela, eds., 1986. *Military Rule in Chile.* Baltimore: Johns Hopkins University Press.

Vanguardia Revolucionaria. 1976. "Programa General de Vanguardia Revolucionaria." Lima: Vanguardia Revolucionaria.

Vargas Llosa, Mario. 1993. *El Pez en el Agua: Memorias.* Barcelona: Seix Barral.

Velasco Alvarado, Juan. 1974. "La Participación en el Proceso Revolucionario." Lima: Ediciones Juventud en Lucha.

Villa El Salvador. 1984. "Acta de Compromiso Entre CUAVES-Municipio." Lima: Municipalidad de Villa El Salvador.

Villanueva, Victor. 1968. *Nueva Mentalidad Militar en el Perú?* Lima: Mejía Baca.

———. 1972. *El CAEM y la Revolución de la Fuerza Armada.* Lima: Instituto de Estudios Peruanos.

Walton, John. 1982. *Reluctant Rebels.* New York: Columbia University Press.

Walzer, Michael. 1965. *The Revolution of the Saints: A Study in the Origins of Radical Politics.* Cambridge: Harvard University Press.

Webb, Richard, and Graciela Fernández-Baca. 1991. *Perú en Números.* Lima: Editorial Cuánto SA.

Weber, Max. 1964. *The Theory of Social and Economic Organization.* New York: Free Press.

———. 1978. *Economy and Society: An Outline of Interpretive Sociology.* Berkeley: University of California.

Wickham-Crowley, Timothy. 1989. "Winners, Losers and Also Rans: Toward a Comparative Sociology of Latin American Guerrilla Movements," in Susan Eckstein, ed., *Power and Popular Protest: Latin American Social Movements.* Pp. 132–181. Berkeley: University of California Press.

Wise, Carol. 1988. Peru Post-1968: The Political Limits to State-Led Economic Development. Ph.D. Thesis, Columbia University, New York.

Zamosc, Leon. 1989. "Peasant Struggles of the 1970s," in Susan Eckstein, ed., *Power and Popular Protest.* Berkeley: University of California Press.

Periodicals

Actualidad Militar
Caretas
Defensa Nacional
El Diario
Expreso
Latin American Regional Reports: Andean Group
Latin American Weekly Report
Marka
Miami Herald
The New York Times
Oiga
La República
Resumen Semanal
Revista Militar
Sí
The Washington Post

Index

Acción Popular (AP), 30, 32, 52, 67,
  103–105
  and 1983 elections, 53–54
  See also Belaúnde, Fernando
Agrarian reform, 2, 10, 16, 17, 29, 46,
  84, 125, 129, 145
Alianza Popular Revolucionaria
  Americana (APRA), 16, 20, 21, 26,
  53, 82, 144
  origins of, 36 (n3)
  and transition to democracy, 30, 32–
  34, 51
  and Villa El Salvador, 104, 105, 107–
  108
  See also Elections, García, Alan,
  Populism
Alva Castro, Luis, 64, 67
Amazonian region, 48, 54, 73, 125
Andahuaylas, 29, 125
Andean Pact, 88
Anti-System Organizations, 16, 25, 51,
  115
AP. *See* Acción Popular
APRA. *See* Alianza Popular
  Revolucionaria Americana
Apurímac Valley, 144
Aragón, Antonio, 100
Arce Larco, José, 21
Arequipa, 30, 53
Argentina, 59, 64, 70, 80, 137, 153
Armed Forces. *See* military
Arms purchases, 44, 48
Army Intelligence School, 16
Artola Azcárate, Armando, 99
Association of Democratic Attorneys,
  123

Ataturk, Kemal, 10
Austerity packages. *See* Economic
  austerity
Authoritarianism, 31
  and Fujimori, 89, 90
  and neoliberalism, 83–88
Autogestión, 54–55, 56, 98, 109
Autogolpe, 89–91
  compared with Russia, 93 (n24)
  See also Fujimori, Alberto
Ayacucho, 120–122, 125, 137–138, 141
Azcueta, Michel, 104, 105, 106

Balance of payments, 42
Bambarén, Luis, 99, 104
Bandera Roja, 120–121
Barrantes, Alfonso, 53, 54, 61, 63, 110,
Barúa, Luis, 30
BCR, Banco Central de Reservas
  See Central Bank
Bedoya, Luis, 30, 76 (n23)
Belaúnde, Fernando, 7, 16, 30, 41, 46,
  47, 52, 56, 61, 83, 137–138, 151
Belmont, Ricardo, 98, 111
Billinghurst, Guillermo, 31
Bobbio Centurión, Carlos, 28
Bolivia, 17
Boloña, Carlos, 80
Brandt, Willy, 98
Brazil, 9, 16, 59, 60, 137, 153, 154
Business sector, 31, 32, 44, 48, 52, 62–
  63, 70, 81, 89

CAEM. *See* Centro de Altos Estudios
  Militares
Cajamarca, 29, 53

About the Book and Author

The dramatic economic, social, and political changes in Peru since the 1960s are explained and linked by Prof. Mauceri to shifts in state power and capabilities. Such issues as the growth of Sendero Luminoso, authoritarianism, the transition to democracy, the debt crisis, grassroots organizations, the shift from developmentalist to neoliberal economic policies, and the role of the military are closely examined.

The book provides a framework to understand the role of the state throughout Latin America that encompasses three key power arenas: internal organization, international relations, and state-society relations. Special attention is given to how policy choices made by diverse political leaders over time have affected state capabilities. The analysis points out the complex ways by which policy choices and structural constraints interact to affect state capabilities in each power arena.

Philip Mauceri is Assistant Professor of Political Science at the University of Northern Iowa in Cedar Falls, Iowa. He is the author of several articles on Peru and the military in Latin America.